Houses of
PRAYER

What they are,
where to find them
and how to start one

Ray Simpson

**kevin
mayhew**

kevin mayhew

First published in Great Britain in 2015 by Kevin Mayhew Ltd
Buxhall, Stowmarket, Suffolk IP14 3BW
Tel: +44 (0) 1449 737978 Fax: +44 (0) 1449 737834
E-mail: info@kevinmayhew.com

www.kevinmayhew.com

© Copyright 2015 Ray Simpson

The right of Ray Simpson to be identified as the author of this work has been asserted by him in accordance with the Copyright, Designs and Patents Act 1988.

The publishers wish to thank all those who have given their permission to reproduce copyright material in this publication.

Every effort has been made to trace the owners of copyright material and we hope that no copyright has been infringed. Pardon is sought and apology made if the contrary be the case, and a correction will be made in any reprint of this book.

All rights reserved. No part of this publication may be reproduced, stored in a retrieval system, or transmitted, in any form or by any means, electronic, mechanical, photocopying, recording, or otherwise, without the prior written permission of the publisher.

Unless stated otherwise, Scripture quotations are taken from *The New Revised Standard Version Bible: Anglicized Edition*, copyright 1989, 1995, Division of Christian Education of the National Council of the Churches of Christ in the United States of America. Used by permission. All rights reserved.

9 8 7 6 5 4 3 2 1 0

ISBN 978 1 84867 806 4
Catalogue No. 1501501

Cover design by Rob Mortonson
© Image used under licence from Shutterstock Inc.
Edited by Nicki Copeland
Typeset by Angela Selfe

Printed and bound in Great Britain

Contents

About the author	5
Introduction	6

Part 1: A survey of houses of prayer

Chapter 1:	Houses of prayer in the Bible	11
Chapter 2:	The House That John Built	19
Chapter 3:	Some prayer houses over the centuries	37
Chapter 4:	The search for contemporary houses of prayer	51

Part 2: Prayers to bless the world around

Chapter 5:	Building a house of prayer	69
Chapter 6:	Fifty things houses of prayer can do	81
Chapter 7:	Prayers that bless the world around	117

Conclusion	129
Books by Ray Simpson	131

*Amid the ashes of Christendom
let homes become divine heartbeats.*

About the author

Ray Simpson is the Founding Guardian of the international Community of Aidan and Hilda which seeks to revive patterns of prayer near ancient sacred sites and in new urban developments. He is principal tutor of its Celtic Christian studies programmes and was team leader of an Ecumenical Partnership at Bowthorpe, Norwich. Ray, who lives on the Holy Island of Lindisfarne, has authored over thirty bestselling books on spirituality and prayer compilations.

Introduction

Christianity began in the intimacy of people's everyday homes. Early churches often met in houses. When Christianity became large scale, and linked to empire, many churches ceased to be homely. Now, as church buildings that lack a sufficient resource base become shells, prayer houses are resurfacing. Like garments made by bespoke tailors to suit each customer, houses of prayer come in every shape and size.

Most religions, in theory at least, encourage all households to pray in the morning and evening and at mealtimes. The custom of landowners providing a room where a praying person can reside has a long pedigree, as have prayer houses beside pilgrimage routes and sacred sites. The practice of creating a prayer room or poustinia in one's own house has spread into Western lands from the Orthodox East. Now, fresh expressions of these ancient traditions enter the landscape. This book tells a story of past houses of prayer and provides a feast of ingredients for emerging prayer houses.

A church leader stayed in my Holy Island home, which is named Whitehouse. 'Our church roof needs repair,' he told me. 'To raise all that money will drain our energy. My heart tells me God wants us to have a house of prayer in each street. This would cost no money and would bring God's blessing to people's doorsteps.'

When churches fade out, the remaining church members fear that the surrounding area will become a wasteland with no Christian presence. In this void, houses of prayer are making their presence felt. Some are making a significant impact; more could do so.

This book explores the idea of such prayer houses; highlights examples in the Bible, the early Church and contemporary life; suggests some life-giving structures and provides a rich prayer menu. The book seeks to relate to faith groups who want to base their work in a house, to Christians who would like their home to become a house of prayer but who do not know how to go about it, and to those who have never thought about it but may be inspired to have a go. It does not wish to drain support from church buildings that still have the capacity to be spiritual homes; rather, it may give such churches fresh ideas. Nevertheless, houses of prayer can attract people who are not at home in a church. This book provides some resources that will ensure the house does not run dry.

The first part of the book sets out the biblical and historical background to houses of prayer, marshalling interesting material from a wide variety of sources. The second part provides practical suggestions for those who are considering setting up or developing such houses. It is full of ideas that have been culled from personal experience or the practical experience of others involved in prayer houses. It is a rich resource.

My story would be falsely engineered if Christianity begins in homes, is taken over by the big structures of empire, and is now returning to homes. The world is too complex for such a simple ending. We are in global flux. Yet Graham Ward, in his book *Cities of God*, suggests that cities might emerge as the primary unit of human society.[1] Although our consumerist, socially atomistic, digitalised society is a constant oscillation of disparate forces and networks, God's Spirit can work in and around them, drawing out the deepest human yearnings, which are God yearnings, for community.

A truer basis of the story is that Christianity began with the natural patterns of the peoples – extended households – and is now returning to the natural patterns that emerge within constellations of forces that make up today's global village. What I think is likely is that within these cities and in their rural hinterlands, houses of prayer will play an increasingly valued role.

---

1. Graham Ward, *Cities of God* (New York: Routledge, 2000).

Part 1
A survey of houses of prayer

Chapter 1
Houses of prayer in the Bible

The first place to be called God's house in the Bible was not, in fact, a house; it was a special place where Jacob had an encounter with God: Genesis 28. There, Jacob had a night vision of a ladder that linked earth to heaven, with angels ascending and descending, in which God promised to bless his descendants. It was what we now call a thin place, because the gap between earth and heaven was thin. Jacob named that place Bethel, meaning 'God's house', and set up a large memorial stone so that others would repair there to pray in days to come. Ever since, all over the world, innumerable homes, chapels and other buildings have been named Bethel – God's house.

In the Book of Deuteronomy, Moses instructs everybody to speak words of devotion to God in their homes each day, when they rise up and when they lie down. He asks parents to teach these words to their children and to write them out and fix them to their doorposts: 'The Lord is our God, the Lord alone. You shall love the Lord your God with all your heart, and with all your soul, and with all your might' (Deuteronomy 6:4, 5). Later in that book Moses stresses the importance of dedicating one's house to God. He instructs officers to say to the troops, 'Has anyone built a new house but not dedicated it? He should go back to his house, or he might die in the battle and another dedicate it' (Deuteronomy 20:5).

Three great yearly festivals were instituted once Moses' people had settled in their new land. Two of these were celebrated in homes. The story of the Passover, which celebrates the angel of plague passing over the homes of Moses' people, allowing them to pass over the Red Sea to freedom, is still retold in the homes of extended families over a meal which includes prayers and blessings. The male head of the household tells the story and blesses the meal. The mother lights candles. All pray. The Gospels record how Jesus gathered his closest friends for his final Passover meal in the house of a friend, to which they were directed by a carefully planned security code: 'And wherever he enters, say to the owner of the house, "The Teacher asks, Where is my guest room where I may eat the Passover with my disciples?"' (Mark 14:14). The Christian Church's greatest sacrament began in a home.

The Jewish Harvest Festival, as we would call it, required each household to make a roofless hut of branches in which they camped out for a week. The purpose was to renew their awareness of God's providence in the past and in the present, through his presence in creation. Centuries later, after exiles returned from Babylon, Nehemiah records, 'So the people went out and brought [branches], and made booths for themselves, each on the roofs of their houses, and in their courts and in the courts of the house of God, and in the square at the Water Gate and in the square at the Gate of Ephraim' (Nehemiah 8:16). Orthodox Jews still do this. In the Jewish quarters of some cities in Britain people erect tents in their gardens during the Festival of Booths. I don't see why Christians can't do something similar. They could invite their neighbours to a barbecue outside their tents. The neighbours' curiosity, if not their piety, will cause them to learn about this 'awareness of God' project.

The political framework envisaged by Moses changed, and kings, both good and bad, ruled Israel. The prophet Elijah had to flee eastwards away from the malevolent King Ahab. He met a widow who had no food for her household. He prayed that her cooking oil and flour would be replenished, and as a result she had enough to feed her household and him. She offered Elijah an upstairs room. When her son became ill and was near death Elijah took him to his room and prayed over him, and he was restored (1 Kings 17). Another woman created an intentional prophet's room for Elisha: 'Let us make a small roof chamber with walls, and put there for him a bed, a table, a chair, and a lamp, so that he can stay there whenever he comes to us' (2 Kings 4:10).

I know people who set a room apart and offer it to a praying person who will reside there for a period of time. This is a kind of prayer annexe. A family man in Norway has created such a prayer space in an attic. He has to climb a ladder to reach it, and family members who do not intend to pray in it are banned!

In the Bible, people would often pray on the flat rooftops that were common in the Middle East at that time. This reminds me of the friend who told me, upon learning I was to make an air flight, 'You will be able to pray better because you'll be nearer headquarters.' The theology may be poor, but the symbolism may be half right. I guess it is less the height and more the space on rooftops that facilitates prayer.

Sometimes we can guess what were good practices in homes from the bad practices that are condemned in Scripture. Kings of Judah, such as Ahaz, made altars on rooftops of the royal palace. The God-honouring King Josiah had these pulled down because they were devoted to false gods (2 Kings 23:12). The prophet Jeremiah declared, 'The houses of Jerusalem and the houses of the kings of Judah shall be defiled like the place of Topheth – all the houses upon whose roofs offerings have been made to the whole host of heaven, and libations have been poured out to other gods' (Jeremiah 19:13). Yet think of the glory of kings and their subjects praying to the true God from their rooftops. The apostle Peter did this, and received a revelation that Christ's Way was for everyone, not just Jews (Acts 10:9-16). This text refers to Peter praying at the sixth hour, that is midday. This reminds us that Christians, like Jews, prayed at certain hours. Midday prayer in houses of prayer is an apostolic practice.

We should not forget that God planned for Jesus to grow to mid-manhood in a home in Nazareth that was also a carpenter's shop. We might call this a cottage industry. Those who cannot wait until tomorrow to evangelise everyone in sight might ponder why this was so. One clue lies in the dictum, 'To work is to pray: to pray is to work'. The carpenter's shop was a forge where relationships with the extended family, the neighbourhood and customers could mature through careful observation, attentive listening, making, playing and praying together. Mary, the mother of all prayer, stored in her heart the divine intimations she received at Jesus' birth, both of the awesome wonder of his call and of the suffering he would endure that would pierce her heart like a sword (Luke 2:35). Wonder and suffering were the core of that Nazareth house of prayer; good workmanship was its hands:

> Jesus, Master Carpenter of Nazareth,
> wield well your tools in your workshop,
> that we who come to you rough hewn
> may here be fashioned to a truer beauty
> by your hand.

Cottage industries can be prayer centres

The writer of John's Gospel portrays seven actions of Jesus as signs of the kingdom of God. The first and the last take place in homes.

Chapter 2 recounts how Jesus' family were invited to a friend's crowded wedding celebration in their apparently spacious home. This went on, as was the custom, for several days. They ran out of wine. Jesus' mother privately informed him of this. Even though Jesus did not wish to draw attention to himself at that time, he prayed over the water in some containers. After this was distributed, everyone thought it tasted even better than the wine that had run out.

This action is sometimes taken to signify that the Jewish rituals are superseded by the more celebratory nature of Christianity. A caption sometimes attached to this story is 'The kingdom of God is a party!' but it is more than that. The kingdom of God is about God transforming the ordinary things of life in our homes.

The last of Jesus' seven signs took place in the home of Martha, Mary and their brother Lazarus. This was in Bethany, only two miles from Jerusalem, which made it an ideal place for owners of spacious quarters to offer hospitality to pilgrims. Their home was clearly large enough to accommodate Jesus and his team. John tells us that 'Jesus loved Martha and her sister and Lazarus' (John 11:5), and their home became a balm for him. Martha seems to have been in charge of household management (Luke 10:38). Mary, who was more contemplative, seems to have owned expensive perfume which was worth a year's wages (John 12:3-8); this she poured on Jesus' feet in an intuitive act of devotion that foresaw his imminent death. Martha made some very astute statements of faith concerning Jesus and eternal life, as recorded in John 11.

Martha and Mary were both devoted disciples of Jesus. Sitting at someone's feet was the usual posture of a disciple who was being taught. In Luke 10:39 we see Mary sitting at Jesus' feet. Perhaps some of the other men and women who travelled with Jesus were also sitting with Mary while Martha was busy preparing a meal. Being hospitable and serving a meal was an almost sacred duty in the culture of that time. Martha was doing a good thing, the expected thing; but Mary chose the one thing that was really necessary: to be with Jesus and learn from him (Luke 10:42).

John's Gospel recounts how Lazarus died while Jesus was elsewhere on mission duties. His sisters had sent a message asking him to come when he became ill, but he did not. When he did arrive, after Lazarus' burial, Jesus raised him from death. This action became a preparation and presage of Jesus' own resurrection. 'Please come,' was their prayer.

'No', 'wait', and only finally 'yes' were Jesus' replies. Yet would Jesus have come if they had not asked? Those who aspire to have houses of prayer do well to reflect on this house in Bethany, and on these three different types of answer to prayer: no, wait, yes.

Jesus spent much time in Bethany during the last weeks of his earthly ministry. He began his ride into Jerusalem on Palm Sunday from Bethany (Mark 11:1; Luke 19:29) and he stayed there the following week (Matthew 21:17; Mark 11:11, 12). It is probable that Jesus spent the last few days before his crucifixion in Martha's home. After his death and resurrection, he ascended into heaven from near Bethany (Luke 24:50, 51).

I have spent time on the site of that Bethany home. In the nearby tomb of Lazarus I prayed for people who were in danger of spiritually dying to have resurrection-like experiences.

Several wealthy women in the New Testament appear to have been the mistresses of their own homes, with no mention of a man: Lydia, Nympha, Chloe, John Mark's mother, the chosen lady (see Romans 16). Other New Testament women were of independent means. Jesus' ministry was sponsored by Mary Magdalene, Joanna, Susanna, and many other women who accompanied Jesus and ministered to him out of their own, personal resources (Luke 8:2, 3). Following the coming of the Holy Spirit, no doubt some of them hosted houses of prayer.

The Christian Church started in a home:

> When the day of Pentecost had come, they were all together in one place. And suddenly from heaven there came a sound like the rush of a violent wind, and it filled the entire house where they were sitting. Divided tongues, as of fire appeared among them, and a tongue rested on each of them. All of them were filled with the Holy Spirit and began to speak in other languages, as the Spirit gave them ability.
> *Acts 2:1, 2*

In the New Testament, prayer meetings were held in private houses: 'Day by day . . . they broke bread at home and ate their food with glad and generous hearts' (Acts 2:46). When Peter was released from prison, 'he went to the house of Mary, the mother of John whose other name was Mark, where many had gathered and were praying' (Acts 12:12). 'On the first day of the week, when we met to break bread, Paul was holding a discussion . . . There were many lamps in the room upstairs where we were meeting' (Acts 20:7, 8).

In the Roman Empire during the New Testament period the poorer people lived in small houses known as *insulae*. This word has the same root as our word 'island'. The home was a safe place in an uncertain world. In cities like Rome, *insulae* were made of brick and clustered into tenements that could be five storeys tall, but in rural regions such as Galilee they were more likely to be built of stones and to have only two storeys.

The home in Capernaum of Simon Peter and his wife was perhaps owned by her mother. Mark 2:4 tells how some people removed part of the roof in order to lower a lame man so that Jesus could heal him. The roof was probably made of turf and mud. The belief that Jesus lodged there is long standing. Archaeologists claim to have unearthed this house, as it was enlarged to include Jesus' room as a chapel, in the fourth century.[2]

A house was not like the house of a Western nuclear family. Although the rooms were small in such houses, there could be courtyards, guest quarters and work areas. In Capernaum and Bethsaida the available stone was basalt – a black porous volcanic stone, poor for construction and very hot to live in. In such small communities, *insulae* were one or two storeys high, often with a grotto dug out below the house for storage or for additional – cool – space.

The *domus* was a type of house occupied by the wealthier classes. It comes from the Greek word from which we get our term 'domestic'. The elite constructed their residences with elaborate marble decorations, inlaid marble panelling, door jambs and columns as well as expensive paintings and frescoes.

In cities, Christians gathered to worship in homes, both *insulae* and *domus*, and the hosts were most likely the pastors. The New Testament letters abound in references to churches that met in homes. In Rome there was one *domus* for every 26 blocks of tenements.

As the *domus* evolved during the early Church era, it had a distinctive floor plan. The 'household' of a *domus* included members of the extended family, slaves, servants and employees. A typical *domus* household could include 50 people. Thus, a whole household coming to faith would be an entire congregation.

---

2. A floor plan can be viewed online. See http://www.capernaum.custodia.org/default.asp?id=5380 (accessed 21 April 2015).

Five of the seven New Testament references to house churches identify them as having female hosts. Acts 12:12 records disciples meeting in the home of Mary, the mother of John Mark. This was probably the first church in Jerusalem. There was Lydia in Philippi (Acts 16:12-15, 40), Chloe in Corinth (1 Corinthians 1:11) and Phoebe of Cenchreae, Corinth's Western Port City (Romans 16:1, 2). Priscilla and Aquila hosted house churches in Corinth (Acts 18; 1 Corinthians 16:19; 2 Timothy 4:19) and Rome. Possibly others included Junia and Andronicus in Rome (Romans 16:7), Tryphaena and Tryphosa in Rome (Romans 16:12), Euodia and Syntyche in Philippi (Philippians 4:2) and Apphia and Archippus in Colossae (Philemon 2).

The apostle Paul sent the greetings of Pudens to his protégé Timothy (2 Timothy 4:21). According to tradition, the church of St Pudenziana (his daughter) is the oldest place of Christian worship in Rome. It was built over a second-century house and reuses part of a bath facility still visible in the structure of the apse.

Early hosts of house churches titled their property to the congregation to be used as a place of worship even after their death. The name given to such a house was *Titulus*. These homes were used as churches for hundreds of years until the Emperor Constantine permitted Christians to erect public places of worship. It is significant that even when the grand edifices of imperial Christianity replaced homes, they were often built over the top of prayer houses. Priscilla and Aquila's home in Rome, on the Aventine hill, is one of the oldest such sites. To this day there is a church in that place. The church and convent of St Cecilia in Trastavere in Rome was built over the home of St Cecilia, an upper-class woman who owned a house on the site and was martyred in the third century. Excavations of Cecilia's Roman house can be toured underneath the church. Even establishment Christianity recognised, symbolically at least, that the home is the heart of the faith.

Chapter 2
The House That John Built

Although big buildings tended to replace homes in the Christendom era of the Roman Empire in Europe, there is an alternative narrative which starts in the east of the Empire and ends up on its western fringes. This alternative narrative has been given the title 'The House That John Built'. It is an imaginative reconstruction, based on scanty but authentic pieces of information, of how early churches with a household feel spread from the region of Ephesus, where John the loved disciple planted them, to the Celtic lands on the edge of the Roman Empire.

Although some scholars have debated whether John the Apostle and John the Evangelist are the same person, the view of Bishop Irenaeus, Bishop of Lyons who died in around 200, that they are has prevailed within the tradition associated with The House That John Built. My friend Andy Raine has created a presentation of poems and stories based on this theme.

What follows is my own selection of early household-style churches within the 'Celtic Arc' that spreads from modern Turkey to Ireland.

Why the title 'The House That John Built'? Jesus reminded people that God wanted the huge Jerusalem temple to be 'a house of prayer for all the nations' (Mark 11:17), but it was not like that. At Jesus' resurrection, the temple's inmost barrier was broken down, as was the entire temple a few decades later. The New Testament word for church is *oikos*, meaning 'household'. Yet once the Roman Empire made Christianity its official religion, churches became prestigious buildings, sometimes dominated by clerics. However, the vision that churches should be spiritual homes has never entirely died, as this verse of a hymn by John E. Bowers and Erik Routley indicates:

> This is the Lord's House, home of all his people,
> school for the faithful, refuge for the sinner,
> rest for the pilgrim, haven for the weary;
> all find a welcome.[3]

---

3. John E. Bowers and Erik Routley, 'We the Lord's people'.

Fewer churches now achieve this ideal. When crowds ceased to attend religious services people perceived many churches to be alien buildings or historical monuments. A perception has grown that historic building-centred churches alienate people who have no church background.

The alternative narrative of Church is based on the idea that John the loved disciple fostered churches in places such as Ephesus in the eastern part of the Roman Empire that were more relationship based than the regulation-based churches of the Latin-speaking parts of the Empire. John's approach was, however, brought to Celtic lands by Irenaeus, Bishop of Lyons, who was mentored by John's disciple, Polycarp.

In the second and third centuries the See of Lyons enjoyed great renown throughout Gaul, as witnessed by the local legends of Besançon and of several other cities relative to the missionaries sent out by Bishop Irenaeus. We do not know how Irenaeus transmitted John's influence, though dispersed members of his large congregation of Celts doubtless played their part. So although in much of the western part of the Roman Empire churches were imperial in style, a different model, more akin to that of John and the East, blew into Gaul, Britain and Ireland from Irenaeus, from the deserts of Egypt and Syria, from Gaul's Bishop Hilary of Poitiers and his disciple, Martin of Tours.

There is no doubt that churches in Ireland, which was outside the Empire – notably the large Columba family of monastic churches which extended to Britain – were inspired by John. They read John's Gospel, the letters to seven Churches in Asia Minor as recorded by John in the first three chapters of the Book of Revelation, and his three general Letters. Whether these were the work of one or two Johns was not an issue for them. They also inherited traditions about his style of doing things. This bond is reflected in the comment of the Irish Bishop Colman of Lindisfarne at the 664 Synod of Whitby, which the historian Bede says related to the date of Easter and 'other rules of ecclesiastical life'. Bishop Colman thought that the Irish approach was the same as that of 'the blessed John the Evangelist, the disciple specially beloved of our Lord, *with all the churches over which he presided* . . .'[4]

This tradition was simpler, pure of heart, more homely. Its spirit, sometimes in a more ascetic form, came alive in Celtic lands through

---

4. *Bede's Ecclesiastical History of the English People*, Book 3 Chapter 25 (my italics).

the cells and huts of the fourth-century Egyptian and Syrian Desert Fathers and Mothers and those subsequently inspired by them, especially through Martin of Tours. The existence of the St John and St Martin Crosses on Iona – the originals dating from the mid eighth century – affirms the strength of this tradition.

I now unfold a narrative of The House That John Built.

John and Mary's house

John was known as 'the disciple whom Jesus loved' (John 21:20). He felt Jesus' heartbeat at the last supper. In art, his symbol is an eagle, which was thought to be the only bird that could gaze directly into the sun without being blinded. John the contemplative gazed into the face of Jesus, the Light of the World. At his death:

> Standing near the cross of Jesus were his mother, and his mother's sister, Mary the wife of Clopas, and Mary Magdalene. When Jesus saw his mother and the disciple whom he loved standing beside her, he said to his mother, 'Woman, here is your son.' Then he said to the disciple, 'Here is your mother.' And from that hour the disciple took her into his own home.
>
> *John 19:25-7*

John's mother Salome was believed to be a sister of Jesus' mother Mary. Although John and his brother James, and perhaps Peter and his brother Andrew, were partners in a Galilee fishing business, there is a tradition that John owned a house in Jerusalem. It is possible that the interview Nicodemus had with Jesus was held there (John 3:1-21).

Six weeks after Jesus made John Mary's foster son, John and Mary were in an upper room in Jerusalem for the Pentecost Festival, with the other apostles. There the Spirit of God fell upon them and many others, like tongues of fire. The new faith spread like wildfire and John exercised a position of influence within worldwide Christianity. The persecution of Christians under Herod Agrippa in 44 AD led to the scattering of the apostles through the Roman Empire's provinces. Irenaeus tells us that John moved to Ephesus, in modern Turkey, where he instructed Polycarp, the martyr bishop who mentored Irenaeus, and died in that city.

John became the shepherd of a household style of Church and had a special relationship with a whole family of such churches, as we know from the letters to the seven Churches in Asia in the first three chapters of the Book of Revelation. The central theme of the three New Testament Letters of John is 'Beloved, let us love one another, because love is from God' (1 John 4:7). Christians were to relate to one another as brothers and sisters in a family. The Roman historian Eusebius (died 340) tells moving stories of John's affection for those he mentored. Tradition says that when John was a very old man in Ephesus he had to be carried to the church in the arms of his disciples and that he often repeated, 'Little children, love one another.'

Many Christians have assumed that John would have taken Mary with him to Ephesus if she had lived that long. A legend, first mentioned by Epiphanius of Salamis in the fourth century AD, claimed that he did. The Eastern Orthodox Church believes that Mary lived in the vicinity of Ephesus but only stayed there for a few years.

Early in the nineteenth century, a German nun named Anne Catherine Emmerich had visions in which she 'saw' Mary's house with crystal clarity and described it in great detail. One of Emmerich's visitors was the author Clemens Brentano who, after a first visit, stayed in Dülmen for five years to see Emmerich every day and transcribe the visions she reported. After Emmerich's death, Brentano published a book based on his transcriptions of her reported visions, and a second book was published based on his notes after his own death.

One of Emmerich's accounts was a description of the house John had built in Ephesus for Mary. Emmerich provided a number of details about the location of the house, and the topography of the surrounding area. She wrote:

> Mary did not live in Ephesus itself, but in the country near it... Mary's dwelling was on a hill to the left of the road from Jerusalem, some three and half hours from Ephesus. This hill slopes steeply towards Ephesus; the city, as one approaches it from the south east seems to lie on rising ground... Narrow paths lead southwards to a hill near the top of which is an uneven plateau, some half hour's journey.

Emmerich also described the details of the house: that it was built with rectangular stones, that the windows were high up near the flat roof and that it consisted of two parts with a hearth at the centre of the house. She further described the location of the doors, the shape of the chimney, etc. The book containing these descriptions was published in 1852 in Munich.

On 18 October 1881, relying on the descriptions in the book by Brentano based on his conversations with Emmerich, a French priest, the Abbé Julien Gouyet, discovered a small stone building on a mountain overlooking the Aegean Sea and the ruins of ancient Ephesus in Turkey. He believed it was the house described by Emmerich where the Virgin Mary had lived the final years of her life.

Abbé Gouyet's discovery was not taken seriously by most people, but ten years later two Lazarist missionaries, Father Poulin and Father Jung from Smyrna, rediscovered the building on 29 July 1891, using the same source as a guide. They learned that the four-walled, roofless ruin had been venerated for a long time by the members of a distant mountain village who were descended from the Christians of Ephesus. The house is called *Panaya Kapulu* ('Doorway to the Virgin'). Every year pilgrims would make a pilgrimage to the site on 15 August, the date on which most of the Christian world celebrates Mary's Dormition/Assumption. Archaeologists who have examined the building identified as the House of the Virgin believe most of the building dates from the sixth or seventh century, but its foundations are much older and may well date from Mary's time.

Sister Marie de Mandat-Grancey was named Foundress of Mary's House by the Catholic Church and was responsible for acquiring, restoring and preserving Mary's House and surrounding areas of the mountain from 1891 until her death in 1915. The discovery revived and strengthened a Christian tradition dating from the twelfth century, 'the tradition of Ephesus', which has competed with the older 'Jerusalem tradition' about the place of the Blessed Virgin's Dormition. As a result of the actions of Pope Leo XIII in 1896 and Pope John XXIII in 1961, the Catholic Church first removed plenary indulgences from the Church of the Dormition in Jerusalem and then bestowed them on Mary's house near Ephesus.

Christians and Muslims have since thronged to Mary's House, for they both honour her as the mother of Jesus. When Pope Benedict XVI visited Mary's House, he said, 'From here in Ephesus, a city blessed by the presence of Mary Most Holy – who we know is loved and venerated also by Muslims – let us lift up to the Lord a special prayer for peace between peoples.'[5] One of the more interesting features of Mary's House is a nearby prayer wall. Pilgrims come from all over the world and write prayers on small pieces of paper that are attached to the wall.

The shrine is still in the care of the Lazarist Fathers, who say Mass there every day. Two resident nuns also recite the divine Office daily. The small, T-shaped stone building consists of a bedroom (on the right) and a kitchen (on the left). The interior is kept simple and austere, fitted only with an altar, images of Mary and candles. The spring that runs under the Virgin's House is believed to have healing properties, and many miracles have been reported. Inside the house are crutches and canes said to be left behind by those who were healed by the sacred spring. The site is wheelchair accessible and provides clean public restrooms.

Macrina's Household at Annesi

The household churches of John and the sometimes homely cells of Bishop Basil, his sister Macrina and the Cappadocian Fathers and Mothers were within travelling distance of each other in what is today's Turkey.

Basil's sister Macrina established a fourth-century family monastery near their home at Annesi. Her mother taught her the Scriptures, household management, spinning and weaving. After her fiancé died when she was 12, she decided to become Christ's bride for ever. As the eldest of ten children, she influenced them for God and established a monastic household.

Basil came back from university 'puffed up with the pride of oratory'. Macrina took him in hand with such effect that he gave up his property and possessions and became a monk. She encouraged Basil to live in a hermitage on the opposite river bank. Soon, this, too, resembled a monastic home, and solitaries came to live nearby.

Basil saw his revival of community as restoring the way that Christ's first apostles lived. His monasteries extended a welcome to married people and children. They sometimes adopted orphans. These were housed separately but prayed together. From the beginning, eastern monasticism was thought of as a movement for women and children as well as for men. Basil became 'the father of eastern monasticism'.

---

5. Source: Fr Robert J. Fox, *Light from the East: Miracles of Our Lady of Soufanieh*. Available at http://www.soufanieh.com/ENGLISH/LIGHT.OF.THE.EAST/Light%20from%20the%20East%20Book.pdf (accessed 21 April 2015).

Lullingstone Villa

In the western part of the Roman Empire, the movement from churches as homes to churches as basilicas accelerated more quickly, but we should not forget that even in Britain the first churches were often in homes. Lullingstone Villa in Kent is the earliest example of a large house that converted some of its rooms for use as a church. It houses the earliest portrait of Christ, who is depicted as a young, clean-shaven man with golden hair. Nearby is a series of figures standing with their arms raised in prayer.

This phase did not last long, and of course the Romans departed, and with them their prayer-house villas.

Martin's White House

The vision of The House That John Built came alive again in Martin of Tours. Martin was born in central Europe of pagan parents. His father, a high-ranking military officer and a friend of the emperor, insisted that Martin, too, become an officer.

In about 360 Martin became a Christian while serving in the army. He was not of the Latin Church; he was a Pannonian. Christ evoked a desire in him to treat each person as if they were part of his family. Martin famously cut his officer's cloak in half and wrapped one half around a freezing beggar. His servant cleaned his shoes each morning until Martin insisted that he would clean the other's shoes on alternate days.

Martin left the army and began to prepare for a life in the service of Christ. He trekked to Bishop Hilary in Poitiers. Both he and Hilary were inspired by stories of Egypt's desert Christians who lived in simple cells, offered hospitality to visitors and were known as Athletes of Christ. Hilary was soon exiled for his faithfulness to the Trinity during the controversy spearheaded by Bishop Arius, who taught that Christ was not the same as God.

During this exile Hilary learned about Basil and his family-style monastic communities and longed that they might grow in the West. At the same time, Martin lived in a cell near Milan and then tried life as an island hermit with a friend. Some years later Hilary returned from exile and Martin joined him. Hilary gave him some farm land at Liguge. There Martin built a Bright White Hut where he might live a life of prayer. His own loving heart and Hilary's encouragement led him to reach out and care for those around. So the huts multiplied, and he drew to him a monastic family.

Martin built a modest school of white stone, and grouped around it were small stone huts in which the men and boys lived. The entire institution was known as a *muintir*, which means 'family, inhabitants or community'. It was looked upon as a religious household.

This white house, which combined the contemplative life with social care, became a prototype that spread throughout Gaul and to Celtic lands across the sea. In the Celtic language the founder was the papa or spiritual father, and his disciples were his *muintir*.

As a result of the mutual bond of affection that developed between Martin's house of prayer and the surrounding people, his spirituality attracted ever wider circles of people. Martin was a healer. On one occasion he was called to the neighbouring diocese of Tours to heal someone who was dangerously ill. The crowds there 'kidnapped' him because they wanted him to fill their vacancy for bishop. Although 'politically correct' dignitaries opposed this, God overruled. At his consecration as bishop, Martin refused to sit on the throne that had become the norm since the Church had adopted imperial customs. Instead he sat on a cow stool. In Tours, too, he lived in a simple hermitage by the river Loire. Others joined him in cells nearby. Women formed a household group in the protection of the city. They became known as his Big Family – Mar-moutier or *muintir*. The area is known as Marmoutier to this day, though only a few ruins of the abbey later built on the site remain.

The Big Family near Tours included recruits from wealthy families, but they no longer possessed personal property or wore showy clothes. They echoed the life of the monks cells of Egypt with one difference – these monks in Celtic lands had a missionary zeal. From time to time 12 of Martin's disciples would hive off under a leader to create a new *muintir*, following the rule of the mother house and retaining a bond with it. Sulpicius Severus, a wealthy legal advocate who wrote the extensive *Life of St Martin*, took some companions, after his wife died, to a villa near Narbonne and started a *muintir* there. His book became a bestseller, and people far and wide conceived a desire to visit the Big Family. These included budding leaders from Celtic lands who were trained and ordained in Rome and then stayed at Tours before they returned home.

Ninian's White Houses

One of these leaders was Ninian. Thirteen years after Martin's death, the last Roman troops left Britain. Britain's leadership fell into the hands of the Celtic aristocracy which had intermarried with Romans. The Christian Church had become an unresourced rump. So Ninian, who had perhaps been a pupil at the school in Carlisle established by the Romans, went to Rome to be trained and ordained a priest. On his way back he stayed at Marmoutier, the famous school of Martin at Tours. Ninian decided to build a *muintir* with a similar monastic family spirit when he returned.

These little communities, composed of a teacher and his followers, grew naturally among the Celtic Christians, for the Celts were accustomed to the clan, or 'relationship', rather than to the imperial form of government of the Romans. The term 'church' was used to describe these places where Christians lived and prayed.

Ninian was reared in what is now Cumbria. Before the Roman troops left, they built well-staffed fortresses along the Emperor Hadrian's wall to keep at bay the attacks from the pagan Picts to the north. The Picts were agriculturalists with quite developed arts: they were energetic and intelligent in trade, cloth-making and battles. By the time Ninian returned, the Picts had overrun Hadrian's Wall.

Undaunted, Ninian crossed over the Solway Firth by boat to establish a *muintir* in their land. Taking brothers with him, he alighted at a small promontory now known as the Isle of Whithorn, and walked to the site now known as Whithorn. He named it *Candida Casa*. This is simply a translation of Martin's 'Bright White Hut', from which today's Whithorn gets its name. According to Daphne Brooke, archaeological evidence suggests his *muintir* could have been an actual daughter house of Martin's Big Family.[6] There is now no trace of Ninian's barns, kitchens, refectory and school buildings, though the cave where he retired to pray is still there.

As time passed, and as more lands were donated, ever more Pictish pupils, shepherds, scribes, gardeners, cooks and lay brothers joined them, and many future Christian leaders in Britain and Ireland trained there. Archibald Scott argues that Ninian's house was unlikely to have been as grand as later eulogisers made out.[7] This view is supported by

---

6. Daphne Brooke, *Wild Men and Holy Places* (Canongate Press, 1994).
7. Archibald Scott, *The Pictish Nation: Its People and Its Church* (T. N. Foulis, 1918).

the references to this White House when Paulinus of York and Alcuin gave money to help sustain it.

Ninian or his followers evangelised Pictland to the north of Whithorn. They divided it into areas. Each had its own small White House. This may at first have consisted of one hermit in his cell who offered a rhythm of daily prayer, and who gathered local people on a Sunday to hear gospel stories and pray. Then others were attracted to live nearby. It is believed that Ninian established White Houses in today's shires of Ayr, Glasgow, Forfar, Aberdeen, Inverness, Sutherland and right up to the Orkney Islands. These formed one family, or dispersed community, who looked to the White House in Galloway as their mother house.[8]

Welsh White Houses of Prayer

So The House That John Built came to Britain through Ninian, among others. These White Houses, or hearths of prayer, were not limited to Ninian's terrains. Many Welsh Christian leaders studied at Whithorn and took this model back to their home areas. The meticulous scrutiny of divergent stories and scraps of information enabled Dr Scott to build up a jigsaw puzzle of the links between Ninian's Whithorn and these new spiritual hearths in what is now Wales.

It is believed that White Houses stretched from Dornoch in the north of Pictland to Ty Gwyn ar Dav among Britons in Wales. Ty Gwyn (Welsh for 'White' or 'Blessed House'), near Whitesands Bay in Pembrokeshire, is a former monastic site with ties to Saints Patrick and David. Other Welsh places named Ty Gwyn include the supposed site of the legendary Welsh parliament that produced the Laws of Hywel Dda, Whitland (*Hendy-gwyn*, 'Old White House') in Carmarthenshire, and Tygwyn railway station at Glan-y-wern in Gwynedd on the Cambrian Line.

The Pict Ternan, who later became abbot of Whithorn, was baptised by one of Ninian's elderly helpers, Paul the Aged. Despite his age, Paul went on to found his own White House by the river Davi in Carmarthenshire. Both Paul the Aged and Manchan (the Little Monk), Ternan's successor as Whithorn's abbot, taught David (Wales' patron saint), who later founded his community at Menevia. Paul sent David to study at Whithorn, to whom David's Christian father sent gifts of honey, fish and dressed stag!

---

8. Scott, *The Pictish Nation: Its People and Its Church*.

Bishop Rhygyfarch's legendary *Life* of David has frequent references to links with Whithorn, though Rhygyfarch also tells us that David was ascetic and contemplative and lived more like the hermits of Egypt. Yet he loved people, and the many 'churches' he founded were little communities where praying, caring people lived. His mother house was on the site of the present St David's Cathedral, not far from where he was born to his mother Non. They carried out crafts, including beekeeping, in order to feed themselves and the many pilgrims and travellers who needed lodgings. They also fed and clothed the poor and needy. The settlement that grew up around the monastery was called *Tyddewi*, meaning 'David's house'. A saying circulated that at his death older people mourned him as a brother and young people as a father.

Other Welsh communities were directly inspired by Martin of Tours, or by the Desert Fathers and Mothers of Egypt. As I wrote in *New Monasticism as Fresh Expression of Church*,[9] according to tradition, the most important Romano-British family in Wales belonged to Maximus, the Roman general who married the British princess Helena. He deposed the Arian emperor, was declared Emperor by his British troops, and established his family at Treves. There the family met Martin of Tours, whose monks were busy transforming the land and peasants of rural Gaul. So great was Martin's influence on their son, Publicius (the Welsh call him Peblig), that after his father was killed by the Emperor of the East, the family settled in Wales and established, at the old Roman fort at Llanbeblig, Caernarfon, an early monastic cell. This was perhaps the first of more than 500 little monastic dwellings.

Some of these attracted so many recruits that they became large communities. Perhaps the greatest of these was at Llanilltyd (Llantwit Major) some 20 miles west of Cardiff. We know that it was great from incidental references in the biographies of Samson and others, and from legends contained in medieval *Lives*.

This house of prayer began with a request that Illtyd would foster a child. According to one story, after his conversion, Illtyd left his soldier's career and became a novice monk under the hermit Cadoc. He was guided by God to make a new home in a green valley suitable for people to live in. The local ruler was so impressed by him that he

---

9. Ray Simpson, 'Celtic Monastic Inheritance and New Monasticism', in Graham Cray, Ian Mobsby, Aaron Kennedy (eds), *New Monasticism as Fresh Expression of Church* (Canterbury Press, 2010).

granted him a wider area of land and asked him to develop a Christian community and school for all ages. Illtyd laid before Bishop Dubricius plans for a community that would combine prayer, leadership training and agricultural development. When they outgrew the farming space that provided for their ever-increasing numbers, Illtyd called the community to prayer and walked to the shore at low tide, when the sea would withdraw a mile or two. He marked a line with his staff and in the name of God forbade the water to pass that mark again. The result was that they were able to cultivate land reclaimed from the sea.

Illtyd withdrew at regular intervals to a cave by the River Ewenny to seek God alone. *The Life of Samson* describes him as the wisest and most learned of all the Britons in the knowledge of Scripture, and in every branch of philosophy.[10] He was also famed as a God-inspired steward of the earth, and he invented a much-improved method of ploughing. 'Seed multiplied and toil met with abundant reward,' says an ancient account.[11]

Professor E. G. Bowen of the University College of Wales, Aberystwyth, believed that the whole of south-western Britain was subject to the influence of the Egyptian Church in the fifth and sixth centuries:

> The persecution of Christians in the Roman Provinces of Egypt and the Near East caused many there to flee to the Desert. At first, they lived solitary lives practicing extremes of hardship. Later, however, some came together in large or small groups for work and worship, and so renounced the world. They were visited in the Desert from time to time by leading Christians in the West and these, on returning home, set up their own monasteries in imitation of those of the desert. Lerins, near Marseilles, and Ligugé, and Marmoutier, near Tours, are cases in point. The pattern of these Gaulish monasteries ultimately spread to Britain. Modern archaeologists have been able to show that the lands around the Eastern Mediterranean, including Egypt, Palestine, Asia Minor and the Aegean islands were in post-Roman times in direct trade contact with south-western Britain. Certain types of wheel-made pottery clearly non-British

---

10. Thomas Taylor, *The Life of St Samson of Dol* (Kessinger Publishing, 2007).
11. A. W. Wade-Evans, *The Life of St. Illtud*, chapter 19. Available at http://www.maryjones.us/ctexts/illtud.html (accessed 18 June 2015).

in character have been found in recent years in Southern Ireland, Wales and South-West England, often stamped with Christian symbols. Along these western sea-routes full monastic life, perhaps starting at Tintagel on the north coast of Cornwall between 470 and 500 A.D., arrived. The monastic pattern spread rapidly afterwards to such sites as Llanilltyd Fawr, Nantcarban, Llandaff, Caldey, Glastonbury, St. David's, Llanbadarn Fawr and other places in Wales before passing over to central and southern Ireland.[12]

Wales is dotted with places named *Llan*. It is thought this word, which ended up meaning a church, originally had the meaning of a family or tribal enclosure. The early little churches were the homes of families.

Irish houses of prayer
Patrick

The House That John Built came to Ireland through Patrick, not by his design, but by Providence working through Patrick's openness to the Holy Spirit in the familial patterns of the Irish tribes. Among many places that claim to be Patrick's birthplace, the north-west coast of what is now England is the front runner. If that is so, he probably went to the major school in the area, in Carlisle. It is possible that he and Ninian were fellow pupils.

This Romano-British youth was kidnapped and became a slave in Ireland, turned to God, escaped and trained as a priest on mainland Europe before heeding an inner call to evangelise Ireland. He won many converts and established churches. Unlike Ninian, it seems he did not visit St Martin's spiritual family at Tours, nor did he at first unlearn the Roman ways. He adopted the top-down Christendom model of the Roman Empire, and appointed bishops who ruled geographical areas. These bishops are listed as the First Order of the Saints of Ireland in a seventh-century catalogue of three successive Orders of the Saints of Ireland. This First Order consisted of bishops who were largely imports – Britons, Franks and Romans as well as Irish – who did not fit the extended tribal family patterns of Ireland.

---

12. E. G. Bowen, *Settlements of the Celtic Saints in Wales* (University of Wales Press, 1954).

This was far from the pattern of The House That John Built. Yet within two generations, a House That John Built style of church had grown, rather like Topsy, and the *muintir* replaced the monarchical bishop as the primary model. These followed the natural tribal patterns of the extended family; their leaders were ordained spiritual fathers from within the tribal leadership. These were the Second Order of Saints. Bishops lived within the monastic family and accepted the oversight of the abba. The Third Order consisted of home-grown hermits around whom grew little communities in remote places.

I can see three reasons why the Roman-style church Patrick planted so soon evolved into the style of a spiritual home. First, Patrick appointed bishops who were open to the Holy Spirit and who therefore adapted to their tribal environment.

A second reason is the nature of Patrick himself as a person who touched the hearts and imaginations of the Irish, even though his framework did not 'take'. Although he knew of only one, top-down model of Church organisation, he served God and people from his own loving vulnerability, and when the Holy Spirit worked in a certain way, Patrick did not stifle this. One story has his first mission team disembarking at Strangford Lough (near Belfast) and walking inland to find overnight hospitality. A swineherd took them to his pagan landowner, Dichu, who, thinking they were bandits, intended to kill Patrick. But he saw goodness in Patrick's face, and Patrick recognised goodness in Dichu. Patrick was made welcome, and, following Jesus' advice to missioners to stay in homes where they were made welcome, postponed his original mission plan. After an initial visit to his former slave owner, Patrick returned to Dichu's Plain of Magh Inis where he baptised and discipled Dichu's household and workers. Bishop Muirchu wrote, 'There he stayed many days; and he went round the whole countryside, and chose priests and did deeds of love; and there the faith began to grow.' So it seems that the first of Patrick's churches were little cells, or houses of prayer on Dichu's homeland.

A third reason why churches that were spiritual homes replaced 'one-man-rule' churches was the women. A late and legendary Life of Saint Patrick translated by Whitley Stokes states that Patrick had five sisters, including the twice-married Darerca who supported his work in Ireland. Liam de Paor thinks that the legendary life of

St Darerca, stripped of accretions, gives us a plausible outline of a female monastic founder who built up a parallel expression of the church to that of the monarchical bishops.[13] She was a woman steeped in prayer, had a male spiritual counsellor, and began to lead a rhythm of prayer under vows in her own home. Then she gathered kindred spirits around her, was tested as an anchoress, and finally became the leader of a community of women in vows, who lived in cells clustered around a place for common prayer.

Patrick recognised needs and callings at the grass roots and responded to them. In his autobiographical *Declaration* he states that sons and daughters of Irish chieftains 'are seen to become monks and nuns', and their number increases more and more.[14]

Brigid

Brigid, Enda (founder of the Isle of Aran monastic community) and Finnian of Clonard are the significant links between Patrick and the next generation of leaders who included 'the 12 apostles of Ireland' and numerous hermits. Brigid was born before Patrick died, and one story has her listening to him preach when she was a little girl.

Brigid's father Dubtach was a pagan chief, but her irrepressible faith was formed in the kitchen where her mother worked as a slave to a Druid. She would lay a spare place at table in case Christ came in the guise of a stranger in need. She would 'pray in' large lumps of butter. If there was not enough milk she would pray over each cow, and even each teat. When she was old enough, she gained her father's permission to live as a Bride of Christ, and joined her mother at the farm. She reorganised it, and the Druid granted her mother her freedom.

Brigid returned to her father in western Ireland, refused to enter an arranged marriage with a famous poet, and gained her father's permission to be prepared for vows as a nun under Patrick's disciple, Bishop Erc. As soon as she made her final vows she began to gather other persecuted Christian women. The bishops recognised a crying need for havens for Christian women, soon realising that these could become much more than that – they became places of prayer, provision and training.

---

13. Liam de Paor, *Saint Patrick's World* (Four Courts Press, 1993).
14. St Patrick, *The Confession of St Patrick*, section 41. Available at http://www.ccel.org/ccel/patrick/confession.txt (accessed 18 June 2015).

Brigid's great hub community was a double monastery for both men and women at Kildare. It seemed common sense, if it was a spiritual home, that men should concentrate on the heavy outdoor work and women should look after household matters. Kildare had a farm. Brigid helped with the sheep and the harvests. The farm provided barrels of apples for lepers and of ale for those who suffered from the cold.

Kildare was the base from which Brigid travelled far and wide in her carriage to establish little houses of prayer, led by women in vows, which civilised the often warring tribes. Although these are not documented, we know that many such existed. St Columba's biographer, Adomnan, tells of a wife in an unhappy marriage who told Columba she would do anything to leave her husband, even if it meant joining a women's monastery in Ireland.

Prayer and hospitality were at the heart of these houses of prayer. Brigid's idea of heaven was a banquet, and she sought to bring heaven to earth through her generous, joyful tables at which music was played. Patrick's grandfather may have stayed at Whithorn, as did Finnian who founded the monastic family at Moville, at the head of Strangford Lough in today's County Down, Northern Ireland. We know from the name Magh Bile – the plain of the ancient tree – that it was already a sacred place, venerated in pagan times. There may have been an earlier Christian house at Moville founded by Finnian's grandfather, a man called St Ailill. This Ailill, a son of Trichem, was a brother of Dichu of Saul, Patrick's early convert.

David gained a love of books from Finnian. Columba was taught by both Finnian of Moville and Finnian of Clonard. Brendan, although fostered by Ita, was taught by Finnian at Clonard. At some stages we have a whole group or movement rather than just an individual.

Ita

Ita established an extended household of prayer at Killeady in County Limerick. She was born early in the sixth century into the family of a Christian chief whose kingdom in south-east Ireland stretched from today's Waterford up to Cashel. As a girl, Ita was devout, capable and beautiful. She became known for the power of her intercessions, and people would invite her to their settlements to cure the sick or to support them when another tribe attacked them. Though she had many suitors, she dreamed that an angel placed three precious jewels in her breast – the Trinity would dwell within her and constitute, so to speak, her love life. She lived for a time in a woodland cell, learned from fishermen to build boats and baptised some Druids.

At about the age of 20, Ita moved westward along the coast towards what is now Youghall, in County Cork. She stayed at Clashmore and also built up churches at Lismore and Ardmoor, where an aged saint named Declan asked for her help and shared his wisdom with her. She cured and cared for many people in the area. A chief further north, whose son Ita healed, offered her any facilities she needed. She asked for some cells where a faith community and a school could grow, to which people could send their children to learn spiritual, poetical and practical skills. Typically, poultry, vegetables and cattle were cultivated. In 523, the three-year-old Findbarr was placed in her care. The faith communities he later established were said to be the origins of the city of Cork. Ita also fostered the boy Brendan, who became famous as the Navigator.

Many came to Ita's household of prayer to confess their sins, even though they knew she would not let them off lightly. They understood that she would require them to make restitution to a wronged person, and so strengthen their ability to overcome weaknesses. She was a soul friend to people at their death.

Ita combined a lovableness with an awesome authority. Her great feats were linked to great fasts, but in a vision an angel told her to lighten up. She became known as the foster mother of the saints of Ireland.

A hymn attributed to Ita has come down to us:

It is Jesus who is nursed by me in my little hermitage.
Though a priest may have great wealth
it is all deceitful except for Jesus.

The nursing I do in my house is not nursing a deceitful.
It is Jesus, with those who dwell in heaven,
whom I hold against my heart each night.

Though sons of princes and kings come into my estates
I seek no gain from them.
I love Jesus better.[15]

---

15. C. Plummer (ed), 'Life of Ita' in *Vitae Sanctorum Hiberniae* (2 vols, 1968).

Although details are sparse, there is no doubt that the early churches in Celtic lands were collections of dwellings. Some began with an individual house of prayer; many became communal spiritual homes. It was not until the second millennium that these were replaced by churches that were not homes, under a diocesan system run by territorial bishops. The Norman conquest of Britain in 1066 accelerated a process that had already begun and imposed a feudal, male-dominated diocesan system. The 1118 Synod of Rathbreasail replaced monasteries with the diocesan system in Ireland. Much, but not quite all of The House That John Built, was lost.

Among the English

As previously noted, Bishop Colman, a successor of Aidan as leader of Iona's seventh-century Irish Mission to the northern English, told the 664 Synod of Whitby, which replaced Irish with Roman ways, that their Irish approach was the same as that of 'the blessed John the Evangelist, the disciple specially beloved of our Lord, with all the churches over which he presided . . .'[16] I suspect he had in mind not only the Irish calendar and monks' customs, but also the homely nature of their places of prayer and work. At Lindisfarne, the simple huts for brothers, students and guests, and the little church at their heart, erected under Aidan, were made of wood, which the Romanised historian Bede thought did not befit the dignity of a bishop.

The Irish Mission did not have prayer houses as such, but they had little prayer cells, or churches, in the homely setting of a village. Aidan had a prayer chapel built for himself on the edge of the king's court at Bamburgh. This approach did not entirely disappear after the Whitby Synod. For example, Cuthbert, the Saxon Prior of Lindisfarne, was granted permission to live as a hermit on Inner Farne Isle. There he built a little prayer house of stone where he could storm the gates of heaven. I sometimes wonder, however, if Cuthbert's island prayer house was in effect the swan song for churches as prayer homes rather than edifices. In the second millennium, as we shall see, the prayer house was the exception rather than the rule.

---

16. Bede, *Ecclesiastical History of the English People* Book 1, Chapter 25.

Chapter 3

Some prayer houses over the centuries

Anchorites' houses

In the second millennium, residents in towns who went to church services sometimes felt unprayed for. The answer some churches came up with was to build an annexe for an anchorite who was paid to pray for every resident in town. Chester-le-Street in County Durham has one of the best preserved of these anchorite houses, which can still be visited as a museum next to the parish church of St Mary and St Cuthbert. The site has been used for worship for more than 1100 years and elements of the current building are more than 950 years old. The oldest surviving translation of the Gospels into English was done here, by Aldred between 947 and 968 when it housed both the shrine of Saint Cuthbert and the Lindisfarne Gospels.

During that period the church served as the centre of Christianity from Lothian to Teesside. The former anchorage, one of the few surviving to this day, is the most complete example of its kind in England. It was created by blocking off one corner of the church in the late fourteenth century, and an extra room was added externally in the sixteenth century. Originally it was on two levels, but the floor was removed at some point to allow more space and light. From 1383 to 1547 it was occupied by six anchorites, each being walled in to the anchorage for life. They would be able to watch services through a squint into the church which looks down on to a side altar, and were fed through another slit to the outside. This lasted until the Reformation, after which the anchorage was occupied sometimes by poor people, sometimes by members of the church. In 1986 it became the Ankers House Museum, one of the smallest in the UK. It shows the conditions in which an anchorite would have lived when it was occupied, and also contains Roman, Anglo-Saxon and medieval items found on the site.

There are records of anchorite houses in England from the eleventh century. They seem to have been at the height of their popularity in the thirteenth, and we can identify some 200 anchorites. There is no sign of decline in the sixteenth century, and anchorites were among the religious who were turned out of their houses at the Dissolution of the Monasteries.

The anchoritic life was embraced by both men and women, though women formed the majority. The men were almost always priests, but it seems to have been unusual for anchorites of either sex to have been a monk, friar or nun. The cell or reclusory usually adjoined the parish church. A narrow window or 'squint' looked into the church and afforded the anchorite a view of the altar. A second window opened on to the outside world (often into a parlour) and allowed the anchorite to converse with visitors. Certain 'cells' had several rooms; some had gardens attached to them. A third window looked into the servants' quarters.

The solitary life of the anchorite could not be lived alone. A servant was required to bring food and remove waste, and to attend to visitors. Aelred of Rievaulx, who wrote an influential 'Rule' for anchorites (addressed to his sister), advised having two: an older woman, for her sober influence, and a younger, to do the fetching and carrying. Julian of Norwich had maidservants (at different times) named Sara and Alice. Material support had to be in place before the authorities would sanction enclosure: anchorites therefore had to be of independent means. They were also the recipients of alms and grants from all levels of society, from the king down to their fellow parishioners.

Walsingham's House of Nazareth

The village of Little Walsingham was a thriving place, located midway between Norwich (then England's second city) and the wealthy town of King's Lynn. Richeldis de Faverches was a Saxon noblewoman who was married to the Lord of the Manor of Walsingham Parva. She was prayerful and full of good works towards local people. Her husband died, leaving her a young widow with a son named Geoffrey.

In the year 1061 Richeldis was taken in a vision to the house in Nazareth where the angel Gabriel had announced the news of the birth of Jesus to his mother Mary. In the vision, Mary asked Richeldis to build an exact replica of that house in Walsingham. According to tradition, the vision was repeated three times, and Richeldis had the Holy House constructed. Her son Geoffrey became its guardian and built a priory around it.

The house came under the care of Augustinian Canons in the mid twelfth century. This simple wooden house of prayer became the focus of popular pilgrimage and royal patronage, until Henry VIII destroyed it in 1538. In the twentieth century, pilgrimage was restored and new buildings erected, although the holy house is more like a chapel than a home. Nevertheless, dwellings for residents and visitors who pray there are sited around the shrine. When I lived in Norfolk I would frequently repair there on a day off. I always met with God there, and answers to prayer came quickly in practical, almost mundane ways.

Count Zinzendorf's one-hundred-year prayer meeting

In 1722, a small group of Christian Bohemian Brethren, who had been living in northern Moravia as an illegal underground remnant in the Catholic Habsburg region, arrived at the Berthelsdorf estate of Nikolaus Ludwig von Zinzendorf, a nobleman who had been brought up in the traditions of Pietism. Out of a personal commitment to helping the poor and needy, he agreed to a request from their leader, Christian David, an itinerant carpenter, that they be allowed to settle on his lands in Upper Lusatia, which is in present-day Saxony in the eastern part of Germany.

The Count's estate manager, Heitz, led the exiles to an old unfinished farmhouse in swampy common pasture ground known as the Hutberg, or Watch-Hill. That is why Herrnhut received the name which was soon to be famous in the land. The exiles, cheered anew, resolved to build the kingdom of God on that site. It was on the high road from Lobau to Zittau, and was used as a camping ground for travellers whose wagons sometimes sank axle deep in the mud.

Heitz was concerned for the refugees. As he strolled around inspecting the land, he noticed one particular spot where a thick mist was rising and, concluding that there a spring was sure to be found, offered a prayer on their behalf. He registered the solemn vow, 'Upon this spot, in Thy name, I will build for them the first house.' He laid their needs before the Grand Old Lady Gersdorf, the count's grandmother and a poet, who kindly sent them a cow. He inspected the site with Christian David. On 17 June 1772, Christian David seized his axe, struck it into a tree and exclaimed, 'Yea, the sparrow hath found an house, and the swallow a nest for herself' (Psalm.84:3, KJV).

The first step in the building of Herrnhut had been taken. But already Christian David visualised a goodly city rising, mapped out the courts and streets in his mind, and explained his glowing schemes to Heitz. As the building of the first house proceeded, the pious Heitz grew more and more excited. He drove in the first nail, he helped to fix the first pillar and, finally, when the house was ready, he opened it in solemn religious style. He preached a sort of prophetic sermon about the holy city, the new Jerusalem, coming down from God out of heaven. The Count himself soon blessed the undertaking.

As the Count drove along one winter night on the road from Strahwalde to Hennersdorf, he saw a strange light shining through the trees. He asked what the light could mean. There, he was told, the Moravian refugees had built the first house on his estate. He stopped the carriage, entered the house, assured the inmates of his hearty goodwill, fell to his knees and commended the enterprise to the care of God. Soon more emigrants arrived. As Christian David went from town to town he urged his friends to come to 'David's City', a 'home' where Protestants could live in peace and comfort.

Herrnhut grew ever larger. Religious malcontents were drawn to it, and discord replaced joy. So the Count intervened. For the previous five years, while Herrnhut had been growing, the Count had devoted himself to establishing a village 'Church within the Church' at Berthelsdorf. Meanwhile, in the village itself, he named his house Bethel; his estate was his parish, and his tenants were his congregation. He had never forgotten his boyish vow to do all in his power to extend the kingdom of Christ, and now he formed the 'League of the Four Brethren', which consisted of Zinzendorf, Friedrich de Watteville, and Pastors Rothe and Schafer. Its objective was to proclaim to the world, by means of a league of men devoted to Christ, 'that mystery and charm of the Incarnation which was not yet sufficiently recognized in the Church.'[17]

Zinzendorf had several methods of work. As he wished to reach the young folk of noble rank, he had a school for boys built on the Hutberg, and a school for girls down in the village; the members of the League provided the funds needed for the undertaking. He established a printing office at Ebersdorf, from which he sent books, pamphlets, letters and cheap editions of the Bible in all directions. As he longed,

---

17. J. E. Hutton, *History of the Moravian Church* (Kessinger Publishing, LLC, 2004).

thirdly, for personal contact with leading men in the Church, he instituted a system of journeys to Halle and other centres of learning and piety. But his best work was done in Berthelsdorf. His steward, Heitz, gave the rustics Bible lessons; Pastor Rothe preached awakening sermons in the parish church, and he himself, in the summer season, held daily singing meetings and prayer meetings in his own house.

While things in Herrnhut were growing worse, things in Berthelsdorf were growing better. Zinzendorf had now to apply his principles to Herrnhut. He had taken the settlers in out of charity, he had invited them to the meetings in his house, and now they had turned the place into a hive of dissent. He taught the exiles to obey the law of the land, to bow to his authority as lord of the manor, and to live together in Christian fellowship. To this end, he summoned them to a mass meeting in the Great House on the Hutberg, lectured them for more than three hours on the sin of schism, read out the 'Manorial Injunctions and Prohibitions', which all inhabitants of Herrnhut must promise to obey, and then submitted a number of 'Statutes' as the basis of a voluntary religious society. The effect was sudden and swift: the settlers changed from a group of quarrelling schismatics to a body of orderly Christian tenants. The assembled settlers shook hands and promised to obey the Injunctions and Prohibitions.

As soon as the Count had secured law and order he took up residence at Herrnhut and proceeded to organise all who wished into a systematic church within the Church. He prepared another agreement (4 July) entitled the 'Brotherly Union and Compact', signed it himself, persuaded Christian David, Pastor Schafer and another neighbouring clergyman to do the same, and then invited all the rest to follow suit. Again, the goodwill was practically universal. 'The whole place,' said Zinzendorf, 'represented a visible tabernacle of God among men.' For the following four months the city on the hill shone with joy. The very men who had previously quarrelled with one another now formed groups for prayer and praise. In the evenings, the entire settlement met to pray and praise and talk together, like brothers and sisters of one home. As the Brethren met in each other's homes, or on the Hutberg when the stars were shining, they listened, with reverence 'to the still voice of that Good Shepherd who was leading them gently, step by step, to the green pastures of peace.'[18]

---

18. J. E. Hutton, *History of the Moravian Church*.

Herrnhut became a major centre for Christian renewal during the eighteenth century. The carpenter David Nitschmann and, later, Count von Zinzendorf, were the first two bishops of the Renewed Unity. Moravian historians identify the main achievements of this period as:

- Setting up a watch of continuous prayer that ran uninterrupted, 24 hours a day, for 100 years.

- Establishing more than 30 settlements internationally on the Herrnhut model, which emphasised prayer and worship, and a form of communal living in which simplicity of lifestyle and generosity with wealth were held to be important spiritual attributes.

Herrenhuters (followers of Count Zinzendorf) established a network in Scandinavia. Various revival movements swept Norway over the following century. These led to the Prayer House Movement. In many Lutheran parishes a prayer house, led by lay people, co-exists with the formal parish church.

Soufanieh, Damascus

The apostle Paul was converted by a blinding light in Damascus. He was healed of his blindness in the home of a man named Judas who lived in Straight Street (Acts 9). That was in the first Christian century. Not far from that house, in the old Christian quarter of Damascus named Soufanieh, further divine interventions came to a home twenty centuries later. The purpose of these interventions, claims researcher Father Robert Fox, was to revive domestic churches and unity among Christians.

In 1982 Myrna, a beautiful 18-year-old Melkite Catholic, married her Syrian Orthodox husband, Nicolas Mazour, who was 20 years her senior. Neither were well steeped in their religion. Nicolas did not want a church wedding, so they were married in their home.

On Monday 22 November 1982, Myrna was accompanied by Alice, her mother-in-law, who still lived with Nicolas. They were at the bedside of Leila, Nicolas' sister, who had been bedridden because of sharp pains which made her scream at times. Several other relatives and neighbours were present. Suddenly Myrna's body shivered, she felt a force come out of her and a Muslim girl screamed: oil was oozing from Myrna's hands. Myrna rubbed Leila with the oil and the pain stopped.

That evening, Myrna was praying when her hands again filled up with oil. It began to dawn upon Myrna and Nicolas that perhaps God was asking something special of them. Myrna placed everything in God's hands. When her mother became afflicted with pain and asked for prayer, the oil appeared again and she was healed. The following day the entire family accepted Nicolas' suggestion that they have a day of fasting and thanksgiving to give gratitude to God for the healing oil. As Myrna was doing housework a few days later she noticed that drops of oil were forming on the glass cover of a cheap ikon of the Virgin Mary that Nicolas had brought back from Bulgaria. They placed it on a plate, then on a tray, which filled with oil. Then Myrna heard a woman's voice: 'Don't fear. I am with you. Open the doors. Don't deprive anyone of my sight.' The doors of their home thereafter remained open all day, and many thousands have walked unhindered into their home. They see the ikon, they pray and they learn about further messages received.

The Virgin Mary is a link between Muslims and Christians. She is the only woman mentioned in the Qu-ran, which regards her as holy. Syria is a cradle of two monotheist religions. Eight popes and an Archbishop of Canterbury (Theodore) have been Syrian.

Father Elias Zahlaoui, a Melkite parish priest nearby, became a confidant of the Nazours from the beginning. In 1982 Myrna received a message that he was an apostle and a shining light. In 2001 he accompanied the author Father Robert Fox to an audience with His Holiness Moran Mor Ignatius Zakkur I, Supreme Head of the Syrian Orthodox Church. Bede Griffiths wrote that the Syrian Orthodox Church is very important for Christendom because it is the one surviving link with the Aramaic church, which was the Mother of Christendom.[19] His Holiness felt that the Christological controversies that for centuries had divided his church from Rome had now been laid to rest, and that the challenge confronting the Christian church can only be faced by coming together in the spirit of our Lord's prayer in chapter 17 of John's Gospel: 'May they be one' (verse 21). One day Nicolas said, 'I think it is the first time in an Islamic country that there has been an ikon in the street (in front of our house), and Christians stop on the street to pray before it.'

---

19. Quoted in Dr. D. Babu Paul, *The Syrian Orthodox Christians of St Thomas*, published online by www.SyrianChurch.org. Available at http://syriacchristianity.info/books/SyriacChristianity_DrDBabuPaul.pdf (accessed 3 June 2015).

Pope John Paul II often spoke of the home as the domestic church, but families need protecting. Even though the doors are always open at Soufanieh and they get tired, they have been protected and nothing has been stolen. Messages are inscribed on the wall. They have been given gifts of humour and special love for each other. Myrna became pregnant and their daughter Miriam said, 'Mama, Emmanuel is inside you'. They named the baby boy John Emmanuel. There is a weekly communal prayer meeting. Conversions and healings continue to take place. Myrna has travelled the world. She has experienced the stigmata and accompanying sufferings whenever the Orthodox and Catholics have celebrated Holy Week and Easter at the same time. People have been led to prayer through the oil manifestations.

During the terrible violence that has devastated parts of Damascus during the civil war in Syria this century, Jesus has brought fresh messages of succour to Soufanieh. For example, 'The wounds which have bled on this land are the same wounds which are in my body, because the cause and causer are the same.' Our Lady of Soufanieh remains a focal point of prayer in Damascus – every day at 5pm the house is open for prayer, and those who come include both Christians and Muslims.[20]

Madonna House and poustinias

In 2012 I visited Madonna House, Combermere, some two hours' drive from Ottawa. It was founded in 1947 by the Russian émigré Catherine Doherty and her husband Eddie, a former Catholic priest. It has two spacious wooden chapels and a refectory and meeting room at its heart, and is surrounded by many individual prayer huts known as poustinias, and farms. Its 200 members live a simple daily routine that begins with a brief prayer service followed by a day of work, and ends with Mass and dinner. Work at the main house generally consists of the day-to-day maintenance of the community, care of a farm, and the sorting and distribution of donations to the poor. Madonna House welcomes guests into its community, allowing anyone to come and join their daily work and prayer routine for varying lengths of time.

---

20. Source: Fr Robert J. Fox, *Light from the East: Miracles of Our Lady of Soufanieh*. See also soufanieh.excerptsofinri.com (accessed 21 April 2015).

The main work of the Madonna House Apostolate is serving the physically and spiritually poor. Through its missionary houses in various countries, staff serve the needy in many ways, from 'prayer and listening houses' to soup kitchens. Formally, Madonna House is a Public Association of the Christian Faithful under the Bishop of the Roman Catholic Diocese of Pembroke. Its spirituality flows from the *Little Mandate*, written by Catherine Doherty, which is modelled on the holy family of Nazareth, which they regard as a community of perfect love.

Some members live in the small, sparsely furnished cabins named poustinias. Catherine Doherty's classic book *Poustinia: Christian Spirituality of the East for Western Man*, first published in 1975, has introduced to countless Western people the idea of creating a sparsely furnished cabin or room where one goes alone with God to fast and pray with open heart and listening soul. The word 'poustinia' has its origin in the Russian word for desert (пустыня). One called to live permanently in a poustinia is called a 'poustinik' (plural: poustiniki). In the book, Catherine Doherty describes the poustinia as 'an entry into the desert, a lonely place, a silent place, where one can lift the two arms of prayer and penance to God in atonement, intercession, reparation for one's sins and those of one's brothers ... To go into the poustinia means to listen to God. It means entering into kenosis – the emptying of oneself.'[21] She promotes the poustinia as a place where anyone in any walk of life can go for 24 hours of silence, solitude and prayer. Ultimately, however, the poustinik's call is to the desert of one's own heart wherein they dwell with God alone, whether in the workplace or in a solitary locale.

In the Eastern and Russian tradition the poustinik is not solitary, but is a part of the local community to which they are called. The poustinik is a servant of God and God's people, in communion with the Church. Historically, one who experienced a call to the poustinia had first, after securing the blessing of their spiritual director, to find a village. They would generally do this through pilgrimage and prayer. Having discovered the village to which they felt God drawing them, the poustinik would go to the elders and ask permission to live there as a poustinik. Permission would happily be given, as Russians were glad to have a poustinik praying for them.

---

21. Catherine de Hueck Doherty, *Poustinia: Christian Spirituality of the East for Western Man* (Notre Dame, IN: Ave Maria Press, 1975).

The poustinik was also available to the people. When there were special needs, such as a fire to fight or hay to bring in, the poustinik would help. And whenever anyone had something they wanted to talk about – a question about prayer, a problem, a special joy or sorrow – they could go to them.

Revivals that started in cottages of prayer

The Hebrides Revival is considered one of Britain's greatest revivals of all time. Following the trauma of World War II, spiritual life was at a low ebb. Then two women began to pray. Peggy and Christine Smith (aged 84 and 82) prayed constantly for revival in their cottage near Barvas village on the Isle of Lewis, the largest of the Hebridean Islands in the bleak northwest of Scotland. God showed Peggy in a dream that revival was coming. Months later, early one winter's morning as the sisters were praying, God gave them an unshakable conviction that revival was near. Peggy asked her minister James Murray Mackay to call the church leaders to prayer. Three nights a week, for months, the leaders prayed together. One night, having begun to pray at 10pm, a young deacon from the Free Church read Psalm 24 and challenged everyone to be clean before God. As they waited on God, his awesome presence swept over them in the barn at 4am.

Mackay invited the noted Bible teacher Duncan Campbell to come and lead meetings. At the close of his first meeting in the Presbyterian church in Barvas, the travel-weary preacher was invited to join an all-night prayer meeting. Thirty people gathered for prayer in a nearby cottage. Duncan Campbell described it:

> God was beginning to move, the heavens were opening, we were there on our faces before God. Three o'clock in the morning came, and God swept in. About a dozen men and women lay prostrate on the floor, speechless. Something had happened; we knew that the forces of darkness were going to be driven back, and men were going to be delivered. We left the cottage at 3 am to discover men and women seeking God. I walked along a country road, and found three men on their faces, crying to God for mercy. There was a light in every home, no one seemed to think of sleep.[22]

---

22. Duncan Campbell, cited on the website of 'Measure of Gold Revival Ministries'. Available at http://www.evanwiggs.com/revival/history/4-1950.html (accessed 3 June 2015). I am also indebted to Gwen Whitmore of Whitby for providing me with her memories on CD.

When Duncan and his friends arrived at the church that morning it was already crowded. People had gathered from all over the island; some had come in buses and vans. No one discovered who told them to come. God led them. Large numbers were converted as God's Spirit convicted multitudes of sin, many lying prostrate, many weeping. At the end of that amazing day in the church, Duncan pronounced the benediction, but then a young man began to pray aloud. He prayed for 45 minutes. Again the church filled with people repenting, and the service continued until four o'clock the next morning when Duncan pronounced the benediction again.

Even then he was unable to go home to bed. As he was leaving the church a messenger told him, 'Mr. Campbell, people are gathered at the police station, from the other end of the parish; they are in great spiritual distress. Can anyone here come along and pray with them?' Campbell went, and what a sight met him. Under the still starlit sky he found men and women on the road, others by the side of a cottage, and some behind a peat stack – all crying to God for mercy. The revival had come. Campbell states:

> That went on for five weeks with services from early morning until late at night – or into the early hours of the morning. Then it spread to the neighboring parishes. What had happened in Barvas was repeated over and over again. His sacred presence was everywhere.[23]

That move of God in answer to prevailing prayer continued in the area into the 1950s and peaked again on the previously resistant island of North Uist in 1957. Meetings were again crowded, and night after night people cried out to God for salvation.

Peggy and her sister and their cottage were a key. When the movement was at its height, Peggy sent for Duncan, asking him to go to a small, isolated village to hold a meeting. The people of that village did not favour the revival and had already made clear their policy of non-involvement. Duncan explained the situation to Peggy and told her that he questioned the wisdom of her request. 'Besides,' he added, 'I have no leadings to go to that place.'

She turned in the direction of his voice; her sightless eyes seemed to penetrate his soul. 'Mr Campbell, if you were living as near to God as you ought to be, he would reveal his secrets to you also.'

---

23. Duncan Campbell, from 'Measure of Gold Revival Ministries'.

Duncan felt like a subordinate being reprimanded for defying his general. He humbly accepted the rebuke as from the Lord, and asked if he and Mr MacKay could spend the morning in prayer with them. Peggy agreed, and later as they knelt together in the cottage, she prayed, 'Lord, you remember what you told me this morning, that in this village you are going to save seven men who will become pillars in the church of my fathers. Lord, I have given your message to Mr Campbell and it seems he is not prepared to receive it. Oh Lord, give him wisdom, because he badly needs it!'

'All right, Peggy, I'll go to the village,' said Duncan when they had finished praying.

She replied, 'You'd better! And God will give you a congregation.'

Arriving in the village at seven o'clock, they found a large bungalow crowded to capacity with many assembled outside. Duncan gave out his text: 'The times of this ignorance God winked at; but now commandeth all men every where to repent' (Acts 17:30, KJV). When he had finished preaching, a minister beckoned him to the end of the house to speak again to a number of people who were mourning over their sins – among them, Peggy's seven men!

Only a few years ago, my colleague Graham Booth took a holiday in the Hebridean Islands. While he was in prayer, Graham was 'told' that he would go to the cottage where the revival started, even though he had no idea where this was. He attended a Sunday morning church service. As he was about to drive off, a man came over to him and asked, 'Would you like to join us for lunch in a cottage where we have a prayer meeting?' Graham went. It was the cottage where Peggy and Christine started it all.

Ffald-y-Brenin

Ffald-y-Brenin is a house of prayer and retreat in the hills in the Pembrokeshire Coast National Park, Southwest Wales. Wildlife, birds, flowers, woods and waterfalls are on the doorstep. This old farmhouse is built of stone with thatched roofs. Everything that happens here is soaked in prayer. Guests are welcome to join with the residents during their daily rhythm of morning, midday and evening prayer.

In 1984, Phillida Mould and her mountaineer husband unexpectedly discovered the crumbling farmstead and established the Trust that would become the Ffald-y-Brenin house of prayer, salvation and wholeness. It was a hard beginning. Then an evangelist named Roy Godwin and his wife joined them and Roy was made director.

One day they sat in the kitchen, itching to 'get back into the real world of an evangelist',[24] when they were interrupted by a couple knocking at the door, saying they had been strangely led to the place and wanting to know more. Godwin showed them around, and before they left he 'invented a tradition' to always pray a blessing over visitors before they leave. A moment of intense encounter with the Holy Spirit took place. Over the coming days, a steady flow of people turned up at the centre, uninvited, drawn by an inexplicable inner prompting. Some of the people were not Christians. Each received a prayer of blessing and was profoundly moved by the Holy Spirit.

Before long, the centre became a place of encounter with God. Prayer spread out to cover the surrounding area and beyond. The pattern became established that a prayer of blessing over visitors released the power of God to work in their lives.

During this time, Godwin, an experienced evangelist, learned some lessons about prayer. The prayer pattern incorporates the thrice-daily rhythm of chapel prayer, ancient traditions such as the *Examen,* and some innovations, such as prayer being modelled around the different courses of a main meal. The numbers committing to this continuous prayer for a whole year grew to 500. The scope of the prayer spread to other nations, with the centre developing a vision for being a place of reconciliation for those in conflict. A vision developed for homes across the nation ablaze for God.

Praying the 'Caleb Prayer' has become an important part of this house's ministry. According to the Bible, Caleb was the chief reconnaissance officer of the land Moses' people were being led into. He advised on the allocation of land. Caleb was given Achsah as his wife. Achsah asked Caleb for one more blessing – springs of water. Caleb gave her the upper and the lower springs (Joshua 15:19). The symbolism is clear – the Caleb blessing is about water in a thirsty land, and fruitfulness. Every day at Ffald-y-Brenin they say this prayer:

O High King of heaven,
have mercy on our land.
Revive your Church;

---

24. Duncan Campbell, from 'Measure of Gold Revival Ministries'.

send the Holy Spirit for the sake of the children.
May your kingdom come to our nation.
In Jesus' mighty name.
Amen.[25]

Although Godwin emphasises that seasons of the Spirit's intensity at the centre ebb and flow, a vision for multiplication of local houses of prayer continues to grow.

The centre connects with early Celtic origins of Christianity in Wales. A sixth-century Irish monk, Brynach, was looking for a place of intercession and prayer for the local pagan community. The 'King's Sheepfold' (Ffald-y-Brenin) proved to be one of those 'thin places' – a joining between heaven and earth where the king's flock could find safety and shelter. From the Welsh Revival years to the present, many others have found themselves written into the spiritual history of the place.

Location is important to the work of Ffald-y-Brenin. One of many stories recounts the experience of a young Australian woman with Welsh family roots. Her Welsh grandfather had been a miner and drunkard who kept the family in a constant state of fear and financial desperation. She despised her grandfather and her land of origin. Yet an experience in the blackness of a nearby mine (now a visitor attraction) opened her mind to the hardships of her grandfather's lightless world, and the darkness of her own unforgiveness. With a symbolic piece of coal from the pit, the woman returned to Australia and established a centre for prayer, worship and repentance that was 'like everything you read of the 1904–1905 revival in Wales'.[26]

---

25. Roy Godwin, Dave Roberts, *The Grace Outpouring: Becoming a People of Blessing* (2nd edition. David C. Cook, 2012).
26. Roy Godwin, Dave Roberts, *The Grace Outpouring: Becoming a People of Blessing*.

Chapter 4

The search for contemporary houses of prayer

People who enter into deep prayer sense the soul patterns where people feel at home.

The House That John Built has been gone for a thousand years, and in this post-Christendom era large Sunday-only church buildings are seldom spiritual homes. There are exceptions: cathedrals, whose closes can gather a community around their place of beauty and daily prayer, continue to draw people. But elsewhere, people search for something that fits their situation, as I did when I became the first ordained leader of the newly built neighbourhood of Bowthorpe, Norwich. Our Ecumenical Partnership was commissioned to 'establish one family of Christians for one neighbourhood'.

Bowthorpe tried five types of prayer house at various times. The first was The Open Door. I lived upstairs. Downstairs was a shop-front unit which we opened for daily prayer and drop-in, lunchtime refreshments and meetings.

The second was almost the opposite kind of prayer house. We formed a Trust which purchased a former farm cottage. Into this moved a contemplative Franciscan Tertiary who was a woman of prayer. She created an oratory. Her spare room was used as a retreat for guests from elsewhere, or for a local person in need. It was not open to the public, but it brought a prayerful presence into the area.

The third kind of prayer house was just like hundreds of thousands of others: a church member's home which was the venue for a weekly prayer and Bible study group.

The fourth kind was called 'The Hut' by local youth. I called it a prayer cell. It was open day and night. We invited a bishop to dedicate it to prayer for the transformation of the unconscious life of the neighbourhood. There were no organised prayer meetings. I and others, including dog-walkers who would never enter a church building, used it often. Technically it was on land that went with the church house, but it was outside its walls and accessed by a public footpath. It was a drop-in prayer place.

A fifth type of prayer space came after Saint Michael's Church School was built. This now has a Prayer Tree on the stairway that all the children pass daily. They are all free to hang a prayer request on the tree.

In due course a new church building was erected. This was heated and open daily, has twice daily prayer heralded by the ringing of a bell, a quiet room, and occasional prayer meetings and vigils. The truth is, however, that places do not remain prayer hubs unless prayer fills the hearts of a core group who accept that this is in some sense their home.

Before I left Bowthorpe I had a life-transforming encounter with God on New Year's Night on the Holy Island of Lindisfarne. It was in a former cowshed that had been turned into an outdoor prayer cell. It reminded me of Bethlehem. As I have reflected on this experience it has seemed to me that God is calling forth many little Bethlehems rather than a few big Jerusalems, so to speak. Bethlehem became an outhouse of prayer, not because it was so designated, but because the people who moved into it, aided by its hospitable owner, were people of prayer who were so in touch with God's will that people who at first had nothing to do with them were also drawn to pray there.

There is a hunger, a search, for such places today. This chapter briefly explores this search.

Eco prayer houses

The quest for fresh expressions of the prayer house leads some to link prayer with eco-homes or eco-villages. Sister Frederique contacted me from her traditional French monastery. She had sought permission to take leave in order to explore how she could offer a praying presence in a place of eco-development. If she were able to discover a way to be part of a house of prayer in an emerging eco-village, she might seek release to do this longer term. She had met a friend of mine at an international religious communities' conference for inter-faith dialogue. He had explained that our Community of Aidan and Hilda Way of Life committed us to relate spirituality to creation care. The Way of Life states, 'We aim to be ecologically aware, to pray for God's creation and all God's creatures, and to stand against all that would seek to violate or destroy them.'

I provided Frederique with examples of how individuals in our Community put this commitment into practice. I informed her that our Retreat House on Holy Island had introduced bio-mass heating and that some residents were involved in a project that might make the island carbon neutral. Lindisfarne was a Nature Reserve, and many pilgrims and retreatants saw spirituality and creation as a seamless robe. However, The Community of Aidan and Hilda did not have as yet a corporate expression of our eco-ideal.

Frederique decided to work at our neighbouring retreat centre, Marygate House, for three months and to pray. She wondered whether she should go on to Findhorn, on Scotland's north-east coast. This is the largest eco-village in Britain, although it is not Christian. I told her about Christine and Tom Sine in the USA, who have a Celtic-style ranch to which students come. I have heard Tom commend the eco-housing movement and call for Christians to be more involved. I told her that Britain had once had hopes of a series of eco-villages planned by the local civic authorities, but I had heard that only one, at Bicester in Oxfordshire, had survived the complex planning processes. I had met there with a group that hoped to start a Christian community in some old farm buildings on the edge of this planned eco-village. They would get involved in the village and provide a praying heart.

I told her about The Chalice Well at Glastonbury, which draws together people of diverse spiritualities, not excluding Christian, who seek to achieve coherence between human heart rhythms and the light within nature. Companions stay in the Garden's retreat lodge which has an Upper Room for prayer, inspired by the legend of Joseph of Arimathea's visit. Its founder, Tudor Pole, wrote of 'the conception of a Universal Intelligence, permeating the whole of Creation and through whom the principles of Life, Love and Wisdom manifest unceasingly'.[27] Some Companions speak of 'the perennial wisdom' of the ancients, as expressed, for example, in Plato's *The Timaeus*. This states that true morality springs from a harmony in the soul and that this reflects the Soul of the world.

I think eco-prayer houses are an idea whose time has come.

New prayer houses near ancient sacred sites

Many ancient sacred sites attract tourists but have become monuments to a past spirituality rather than entrances to a living spirituality. Now, however, Christians are being drawn to establish houses of prayer nearby. Two examples of these in Ireland are God's Cottage at

---

27. From an article in *The Chalice*, the magazine of Companions of Chalice Well, Glastonbury.

Glendalough and the larger Prayer House at Clonmacnoise, named *Cluain Chiaráin*.

Glendalough, nestling among two lakes and seven valleys in Ireland's Wicklow Mountains, attracts ever more visitors who come for the beauty of nature and the world's best-preserved remains of a Celtic and medieval monastic village. A few years ago I asked myself whether ice cream cones were all that was on offer to today's soul travellers. Not so now. On the right of the monastery buildings, as pilgrims wend their way to the Upper Lake, is 'God's Cottage', a geo-thermally heated place of prayer and a spiritual resource shop. On the stone altar are carved the prophet Isaiah's words: 'You will rebuild the ancient ruins, build on the old foundations'. My sister Sally and I prayed there. We learned that it is the vision of Father Thaddeus Doyle and a Trust which recently purchased it from donations.[28]

Some years ago I met the parish priest of Ballinasloe, Father Paddy Kenney. He was grieved that so many tourists came to the ancient monastic site at Clonmacnoise but no longer did anyone live and pray there. He set up a Trust in the hope of purchasing a nearby property and turning it into a house of prayer. Shortly before he died there was still insufficient support to bring this into being. He asked my Community of Aidan and Hilda to pray for it, which we did. Father Paddy managed to buy a cottage and build a small chapel and retreat centre next to it, which he called St Ciarán's prayer centre (*Cluain Chiaráin*).

Sean Ascough, the recent leader of Youth 2000 in Ireland, made a pilgrimage to Clonmacnoise in 2004 and sensed a powerful surge of grace during an open-air Mass that moved him to tears. Father Paddy invited Youth 2000 to use his new centre for prayer events. After one event in 2006, Sean and a co-leader named Paul Rooney felt drawn to stand on the ditch just across from the prayer centre looking over the neighbouring field. 'That bit of ground would be very helpful to the prayer centre,' he thought, 'as the centre doesn't have much land around it, and young people need space.' Paul agreed. They would call it 'Mary's Field' – but it was not for sale. Three months later a For Sale notice went up, but they lacked the money to buy it. Generous gifts came, but when the deadline arrived for signing a contract they were 29,000 euros short. On the day it seemed they would lose the contract, they opened the post. It contained 29,000 euros!

---

28. You can read all about it at www.glendaloughprayercentre.org (accessed 24 April 2015).

On the feast of St Patrick 2007 they began a monthly night vigil every third Friday at the prayer centre from 10pm to 3am to pray for the renewal of faith at Clonmacnoise and for the re-evangelisation of Ireland. Youth 2000 up to that point had held its annual summer festival at Knock, but it had become necessary to find an alternative venue. Clonmacnoise seemed the obvious place now, but to turn the tiny prayer centre and two rough fields into a suitable site for more than a thousand young people was a mammoth task.

A team of older volunteers from Catholic Charismatic Renewal prayer groups and church communities helped them set up the site and service the conference. Never before had they seen so many conversions and graces. It was truly holy ground. Sean felt that what was happening there was a prophetic sign for the whole of Ireland and the wider Church. For example, the deep desire for holiness and the special lengths to which the monks and community members were prepared to go in order to come close to God. The Eucharist was the centre of life and so was Sacred Scripture. There was a special love for the Psalms, the Liturgy of Hours and *Lectio Divina*. It was a focus for reconciliation and pilgrimage. The fervent pursuit of truth through study and learning was central to the life and growth of the former monastery, and this could be pursued again. Sean shared with me his vision of an archipelago – small new groups of Christians, each with their own charism, each encouraging the others without a spirit of competition, who will emerge around the great River Shannon at Clonmacnoise in their little houses of prayer.

The hidden house of prayer

There is such a thing as a house of prayer that never advertises itself. Such a house is like the pearl of great price in Jesus' parable. It lies buried in a field. When someone discovers it, they sell everything and buy the field in order to have the pearl. The hidden house of prayer has drawing power.

An example of such a house of prayer was the Transfiguration Community which existed at Rosslyn, near Edinburgh, for nearly half a century. In 1965 Roland Walls, the Scottish Episcopal priest at Rosslyn Chapel, Edinburgh, formed a little ecumenical, Celtic-style fraternity that was based in his parsonage. Soon afterwards they acquired a plot of land 100 yards away in Manse Road, in the middle of a row of substantial but ordinary houses. On this plot stood the Abernethy Rooms, a building that had been given to Rosslyn for the benefit of miners and their families by Lady Abernethy in 1901. It was constructed out of wood with corrugated iron sheeting on the walls and roof. It had quite a spacious garden.

They chose a Gaelic name for their residence, *Comaraich*, which means 'Sanctuary'. Soon they used the house, which they christened The Tin Tabernacle, as the entrance place of hospitality. Its door was always open and meals were made there. Any visitor could have a meal or stay overnight. They turned the garden into a silent enclosure and erected wooden huts. The largest hut was a chapel and the others were the brothers' cells. A sister, Patty, lived in her own house not far away. If a visitor was observed in The Tin Tabernacle, sooner or later one of the brothers would speak or eat with them.

Some members of the community did part-time paid work, including John Halsey, an aristocrat who for a time worked as a miner, but they all gathered together for communal morning, midday and evening prayer. Visitors who observed the silence could join in these chapel prayers, which included Scriptures, psalms, liturgical and free prayer. For members, the daily prayer was complemented each month by a 24-hour silent retreat somewhere away from the premises, each on their own. Every day, members would say a prayer drawn from one of the communities that had inspired them, such as Taizé, and this Prayer of Abandonment from Charles de Foucauld of the Little Brothers of Jesus:

> Father, I abandon myself into your hands:
> do with me what you will.
> Whatever you do I will thank you.
> Let only your will be done in me, as in all your creatures,
> and I'll ask nothing else, my Lord.
> Into your hands I commend my spirit;
> I give it to you with all the love of my heart,
> for I love you, Lord, and so need to give myself,
> to surrender myself into your hands
> with a trust beyond all measure,
> because you are my Father.

Some question whether a hermit calling is relevant to the needs of those who live nearby. Does it not insulate the hermit from connection to the world around? True hermits become so free from the surface ego life that they embrace their humanity. No longer distracted, they are now connected at the deepest level with the people and the place in which their house is set. The story of this community, which has now almost closed, is told in *A Simple Life: Roland Walls & the Community of the Transfiguration* by John Miller.[29]

Christian ashrams

A Christian ashram adapts the popular Hindu style of a common contemplative home and invites Jesus to be its host. The father of the Christian ashram movement was Italian Jesuit Roberto de Nobili, a Christian missionary to India who decided to overcome the cultural obstacles to his mission by adopting the various forms of a Hindu *sannyāsi*. In Hindu philosophy, four age-based life stages are known as *Brahmacharya* (single student), *Grihastha* (householder), *Vanaprastha* (retired forest dweller) and *sannyasins* (traditionally thought of as men or women in the late stages of life who renounce worldly attachments to devote themselves wholly to the spiritual life). Young *Brahmacharis* may also skip the other stages and devote themselves to purely spiritual pursuits. A *sannyasi* (male) or *sannyasini* (female) is an ascetic renunciate with parallels in other traditions.

Roberto de Nobili was followed in this by Brahmabandhab Upadhyay, who was not a missionary but an Indian Brahmin who converted to Catholicism. Two French priests co-founded the Saccidananda Ashram (also called Shantivanam) in 1938 at Tannirpalli in Tiruchirapalli District. Upadhyay had an influence on Bede Griffiths, who co-founded Kurisumala Ashram with Francis Mahieu and who took over leadership of the Saccidananda Ashram after Monchanin's death.

This ashram, in Tamil Nadu in southern India, continues following the death of Bede Griffiths and is a centre of prayer and meditation for many thousands of people. Its life is based on the Rule of St Benedict and on the teaching of the monastic Fathers of the Church, but they also study Hindu doctrine (*Vedanta*) and make use of Hindu methods

---
29. Saint Andrew Press, 2014.

of prayer and meditation such as yoga. In externals, the community follows the customs of a Hindu ashram, wearing the saffron colour robe of the *sannyasi* (*kavi*), sitting on the floor and eating with the hand. In this way, they seek to preserve the character of poverty and simplicity which has always been the mark of the *sannyasi* in India. A distinctive feature of the life is that each monk lives in a small thatched hut which gives him a great opportunity for prayer and meditation and creates an easy atmosphere of solitude and silence. Two hours are specially set apart for meditation: the hours of sunrise and sunset, which are traditional times for prayer and meditation in India. The community meets for prayer three times a day, in the morning after meditation, when the prayer is followed by the celebration of the Holy Eucharist, at midday and in the evening. At this prayer time they have readings from the Vedas, the Upanishads and Bhagavad Gita as well as from Tamil classics and other Scriptures, together with psalms and readings from the Bible, and they make use of Sanskrit and Tamil songs (*Bhajans*) accompanied by drums and cymbals. They also make use of *arati*, waving of lights before the Blessed Sacrament, and other Indian customs, which are now generally accepted in the Church in India.

For those who seek to become permanent members of the community, there are three stages of commitment to the life of the ashram. The first is that of *sadhaka* – that is the seeker or aspirant. The second is that of *brahmachari* – that is one who has committed himself to the search for God, who need not remain permanently attached to the ashram. The third is that of *sannyasi* – one who has made a total and final dedication; when they receive the *kavi* they are committed for life to the search for God in renunciation of the world, of family ties and of themselves, so as to be able to give themselves entirely to God. This, however, need not involve a permanent stay in the ashram; in accordance with Indian traditions, *sannyasins* are free to wander or go wherever the Spirit may lead them.

Many other Christian ashrams now exist in India. These include Christa Prema Seva Ashram (located in Shivajinagar and founded in 1927 by Anglican John 'Jack' Winslow), Jyotiniketan Ashram (in Bareilly) and Christi Panti Ashram (in Varanasi). Other ashrams include Sat Tal Ashram founded by Methodist missionary E. Stanley Jones. His style of ashram, which was transplanted to the USA, seeks to help all people deepen their experience of God in daily living.

The word ashram – meaning 'retreat' – is a word that comes from Sanskrit. Following his personal retreat experience in India, E. Stanley Jones recognised the value of a time for alternating discipline and rest, seeking spiritual health and renewal. The Ashram creates space and time for learning, prayer, reflection, fellowship and rest. This is rooted in the practice of listening for God. Each day, a gifted and qualified Bible teacher provides Scripture-based lessons for reflection.

The aim of those in Christian ashrams is to unite themselves with this Hindu tradition of renunciation of the world in order to seek God or, in Hindu terms, 'liberation', as Christian monastic *sannyasins*. Though the ashram's primary call is to discover 'the kingdom of God within', it is also deeply proactive to the cry of the poor in their milieu through the words of Jesus: 'Just as you did it to one of the least of these who are members of my family, you did it to me' (Matthew 25:40). One ashram runs a home for the aged and destitute, is involved in educating the children of the poorest, provides milk to children under three years of age to fight malnutrition, and repairs and builds houses for the homeless. Thus the ashram gives free boarding, lodging and medical care to 25 elderly and destitute. Poor and deserving children receive books, school uniforms and clothes every year.

Prayer sheds

Emmaus House in Edinburgh was purchased by Andrew Bain and a colleague as a place of daily prayer and hospitality. Andrew moved out of parish ministry for a time to do this. The chapel is a new shed they have erected in the garden. People who have given up on parish churches love to come there. This is a living embodiment of our theme.[30]

'Up with the parallel universe! Up with denominations who recognise the value of the shed revolution' emailed Richard Adams, a Community of Aidan and Hilda coordinator for North Wales, from Anglesey (Ynys Mon) in Wales. It came on the day the media announced a new coastal walk from one end to the other of the Welsh coastline. Numerous places on or near this walk have Christian roots, which started with one person building a cell near a well and praying in it. Richard continued:

---

30. More information is available at http://www.emmaushouse-edinburgh.co.uk/ (accessed 24 April 2015).

I thought your blog about churches growing from one person praying in a shed, as it were, was particularly relevant to Anglesey. The pattern of church buildings here is based on that old Celtic cell or Llan pattern, but the overlay of the parish system has partially crippled that approach and ossified the network. Some churches here are rediscovering that role of being a prayer centre open to all. I'm praying (and nudging clergy and others!) to spread the work wider. And the general move of the Spirit across Wales seems to be about prayer points in localities, praying for that locality. My summer house will soon be fit for use by passers-by with a prayer urge! We've put in new windows and door and the roof has been relaid, so it's fully water- and wind-proof. Once the last boxes have gone and I've laid a new floor and painted it, all will be ready. I hope it will be another small link in the growing chain of local prayer places across the island.

In Australia, too, the Christian men's shed movement is now big.

Declining monasteries recycled as prayer houses

In countries like Britain, religious communities who cannot replace their aging members with younger people in vows often recycle their building as a house of prayer. These may be staffed by a mix of nuns or monks, volunteers and paid helpers.

Saint Joseph's in Formby, near Liverpool, thrives on this basis. It is owned by The Poor Servants of the Mother of God, an international congregation of Catholic Sisters that was founded in 1872 by Frances Taylor. It is used by people of diverse churches and none who come for quiet days, retreats, creative art classes or special prayer events. The sisters help people who may have only a seed of faith to take first steps in prayer. 'Do you find personal prayer difficult?' a free leaflet asks. 'Do you find the whole idea of prayer childish? Are you still doing what you more or less did as a child? Have you given up in despair? Well then, try this dual exercise for size!' The first exercise is as follows:

> When you wake up each morning give God two seconds. Say to
> God in your heart and mind and really mean it: 'Jesus I offer my

day to you'. Then get up and get on with all that the day brings. You have offered the whole day to God, so unless you are consciously breaking God's commandments then every single thing you do is a prayer.

Community of Aidan and Hilda households

Members of the dispersed Community of Aidan and Hilda who own or lease a house may, with the agreement of the household members, apply to become a Community of Aidan and Hilda House. Before they apply, they draw up a Way of Life for the household. This sets out how the household aims to corporately express the Three Life-giving Principles of Simplicity, Purity and Obedience, and the Ten Waymarks of the Community Way of Life. These include a rhythm of prayer, work and recreation, intercession, study, simple lifestyle and service to the poor.

A minimum is envisaged of daily prayer, weekly corporate meals and sharing of faith journeys, a specific outreach and the hosting of group meetings. The Community supports the house by providing a soul friend to the household, and the household gives an annual account to a community guardian who visits and rededicates the house.

Prayer rooms

It is normal for hospitals to have a chapel or prayer room. Certain schools also have them. Occasionally a big modern centre will offer its customers a prayer room. Good capitalists know their markets. They realise that customers know that humans do 'not live by bread alone' (Matthew 4:4); everyone has a spiritual hunger.

The manager of a new city-centre shopping mall in Ireland approached his local Catholic priest and Protestant minister. He offered to provide a prayer room free of charge and begged them to run it. This gave them a hard choice that would involve much extra work. Eventually they concluded that their dwindling congregations were mainly on Sundays, and this was an opportunity not to be missed. So they agreed to run the prayer room six days a week on the condition that it was closed on Sundays.

Football and other sports clubs sometimes have chaplains. Cyclists and motorcyclists sometimes hold dedication services. In Ireland it is not unusual for the local boxing club to be run by the church. A prayer room, or even a prayer corner, is a natural adjunct of these traditions. The prayer room typically offers a calming space, a visual focus, and the opportunity to light a candle or leave a written prayer.

24/7 prayer rooms

In September 1999, a small group of students in southern England accidentally started the first 24/7 prayer room. They just wanted to see what would happen if they prayed non-stop for a month. To their amazement, young people from local schools as well as Christians turned up and they continued for three months! Word spread like wildfire through the internet, and the 24/7 prayer movement began to span the globe.

Creating a temporary monastery for one week of 24/7 prayer, on a rota basis, consisting of intriguing prayer methods such as music, intercession boards, tweets, silence, dance and crafts is one thing. Sustaining daily prayer is another. So the idea of boiler rooms developed. The boiler room fuels a building; it is the source of its heat. These are spiritual boiler rooms. Anyone would be welcome in the boiler rooms so that social provision and chit-chat was interspersed with prayer activities. One problem, however, is that they can be magnets for particularly needy people, and the rest get worn down. So people began to explore ancient prayer disciplines in order to find prayer frameworks that were sustainable. Now, here and there, a few people live in or around a prayer room that has an advertised pattern of formal or informal prayer times.

People involved in 24/7 prayer like to quote Isaiah 62:6, 7:

> Upon your walls, O Jerusalem,
> I have posted sentinels;
> all day and all night
> they shall never be shaken.
> You who remind the Lord,
> take no rest,
> and give him no rest
> until he establishes Jerusalem
> and makes it renowned throughout the earth.

In the UK, the number of prayer rooms rose steadily. In the first five months of 2011, for example, more than 200 prayer rooms registered on the 24/7 website, plus more than 100 across Ireland, as well as more than 50 UK prayer spaces in schools. These can involve the simple, honest prayers of people who would not even call themselves Christians. The story of the birth of this 24/7 prayer movement is told in *Red Moon Rising* by Pete Greig and Dave Roberts.[31]

Established in the autumn of 2001, the Greater Ontario House of Prayer (GOHOP) has served the Body of Christ across Southern Ontario, stirring up prayer and developing and equipping prayer leaders and initiatives. Through training, consultation and coming alongside, GOHOP helps congregations find and expand their prayer language and weave more prayer into the life of their congregation. With a staff of dedicated prayer missionaries and volunteers, GOHOP coordinates and hosts approximately 20 hours of prayer every week, including young adult prayer cells and evening discipleship groups. During my visit to them they brought a prayer van into the main street into which shoppers could come to be prayed for or to leave a written prayer request which would be offered up in the prayer house.

A Light in Every Street

A generation ago, the Evangelical Alliance promoted the idea of A Light in Every Street. Some churches, including my own, took this up with serious intent. Even in the toughest housing estates you can usually suss out someone in a street who is savvy, who knows what's going on, to whom people talk – the wise mother or friendly uncle figure, perhaps. Someone with a hospitable, understanding heart who is bigger than the petty feuds or gang warfare that can tear a community apart. Suppose someone like that is also a person of prayer, who lets their house be an interface rather than a fortress for the area? Then there is a light in that street.

A street in another area may be a safe, suburban row of semi-detached houses where commuters come home and keep themselves to themselves. Yet if someone in that row were to have a little inner space, imagination and motivation, they might move the logjam. They

---
31. Pete Greig and Dave Roberts, *Red Moon Rising* (Kingsway Publications, 2004).

might make a list of the names of their fellow residents, start to pray for them on a daily rota and invite them to a barbecue, for example.

In our church we made a map which included every street. Then we identified those streets in which lived a church member who might be approached to pray for everyone in their street. That was the minimum. After that they could, if the Spirit moved them, branch out a bit more. They might put slips through their neighbours' letter boxes inviting them to return any prayer requests. Or they might inform them that they are prayed for at a certain time each week, or each day.

That left half the streets without a designated Light. If we knew of a Christian from another church who lived in a street, we invited them to become a Light. Then we realised that many people pray, although they would not call themselves committed Christians, and some of them are people of goodwill. We could ask them to look out for anyone in need and let one of us know, so that we could pray for or visit that person.

Street Lights turned on in unlikely places. Among such Street Lights, some might be willing that their home, not just themselves, might become the Light. If they share the house with family or friends, these people need to be in agreement to this. Where there is agreement, then prayer meetings may be held. The individual Lights become prayer houses of light.

Table churches and new monastic houses

Texas has mega churches. However, the Spiritual Life Technology Team at Gateway Church in Dallas/Fort Worth, has launched an internet resource that guides members of large churches as to how they can form small, intimate groups who meet midweek to eat and pray around a table. In contrast to this marketing formula is Safespace in Telford, which has the reputation of being the least churchgoing town in the UK. The members of this new monastic group feel called to share their lives with those who live around them through hospitality and witness. They seek to live out the three values (or DNA) of pilgrimage, mission and community through rhythms of daily prayer, Scripture reading and meditation, accompanied by the weekly pattern of meeting around the meal table and breaking bread together.

Others do it differently. Formats vary. The rhythm of prayer and Scripture reading can be alternated. Once a month an extended gathering might discuss a prepared topic or meditate on one core value in a Rule of Life.

Many families experience real challenges in setting good boundaries when raising children, and also as adults when making good decisions for their own sakes. Discussing and helping to guide each other as families and individuals can encourage the making of common guidelines. Making a meal in an extended household is in itself a great way of sharing life together. Fair trade is important, and a healthy diet. This format lends itself to new monastic networks who may base their purchasing on a shared purse. Time is at a premium for many, so this works best among people who live or work near each other. Flexibility is important. Teenage members of a family should be free to come or not, but everyone who is fit and able is encouraged to take responsibility for preparing an occasional table meal.

Many new monastic expressions revolve around a home or a group of people who live near to one another and become an intentional community of prayer and service. 'The renewal of both the Church and Society will come through the re-emergence of forms of Christian community that are homes of generous hospitality, places of challenging reconciliation and centres of attentiveness to the living God.'[32]

---

32. Brother Samuel SSF (taken from a podcast, available at mootuk.podbean.com (accessed 25 April 2015) and quoted in Ian Mobsby and Mark Berry, *A New Monastic Handbook: from vision to practice* (Canterbury Press, 2014).

Part 2
Prayers to bless the world around

Chapter 5
Building a house of prayer

People cannot learn to pray everywhere all the time until they have first learned to pray somewhere some of the time. 'Wisdom has built her house...' says the Scripture (Proverbs 9:1).

The building of a house of prayer starts with wise foundations. 'Everyone then who hears these words of mine and acts on them will be like a wise man who built his house on rock. The rain fell, the floods came, and the winds blew and beat on that house, but it did not fall, because it had been founded on rock,' said Jesus (Matthew 7:24, 25). In contrast, the house built on shifting sands fell down (verse 27).

What does this mean in the context of a house of prayer? What are the faulty foundations we need to avoid and the solid foundations we need to put in place?

Different styles of house require different foundations. There could be a house of prayer whose owners or tenants permit it to be used for a weekly prayer meeting without that impinging on the way they live for the rest of the week. The ideal, however, is that a house of prayer is itself a sign.

So let's start with the shifting sands and a health warning. 'The road to hell is paved with good intentions,' goes the saying. We hope for wisdom and godliness but unless we allow our motives to be sifted in solitude we will end up imposing prayer houses that are alienating. We have to let go of the control syndrome that flourishes when our lives are too cluttered, and when we carry out projects that are the products of a mindless Christian treadmill. Wait until the initiative comes from the deep heart's core.

Don't start with a holy bubble, for the bubble bursts more quickly than sands can shift. A falsely pious, holier-than-thou group that uses religious language which alienates neighbours is doomed from the start. That is a Narcissus house. The pious group looks out and sees a reflection of itself – it does not see the hurts and hopes, the history and struggles, the mindsets and connecting points in the people who live around them. Avoid the shifting sands of judgemental attitudes. 'Be yourself; everyone else is already taken,' wrote Oscar Wilde. Allow the neighbours you pray for to be themselves. As Henri Nouwen reminds us in his book *Reaching Out*, hospitality of the heart is not a subtle invitation to the other to become like us, so that we get our way. It is an invitation to them to sing their own songs, dance their own dances, and be who they truly are.

Avoid the surface sands of a dull routine that is paper thin because it flows out of no deep wellspring. You become stale, the neighbours become bored, and the ground shifts from under your feet. Creative routine is a different matter.

Avoid the shifty sands of over-driven prayer programmes that make people feel they are being got at, pressurised, like units in a marketing exercise. You burn out and they get out. To engineer cheap or pressurised or alienating forms of prayer will bring the house into disrepute.

What are good foundations? The house of Wisdom referred to in Proverbs 9:1 is built upon seven pillars. Without pillars the structures of the house would not survive the weight subsequently put upon them. The number seven may simply mean that the house had the right or perfect number of pillars. However, as people have meditated on the seven pillars they have associated these with sources of wisdom that were significant for them. Some have linked them with the seven days of creation and the wisdom we can gain from each of these aspects of God's work, or with the seven-branched candlestick of the Tabernacle (Exodus 25:37). Classical scholars have linked them with the seven liberal arts of a good education. Others have suggested that the schools of the prophets trained young people up in seven areas of divine knowledge and skills. Christians may associate them with the seven qualities of the Spirit that come with the Messiah (Isaiah 11:2, 3), which the church formulated as wisdom, understanding, counsel, knowledge, fortitude, piety, and awe of God.

Values

I think the pillars of a house of prayer consist of its values, practices and structures. It is useful to draw up a simple values or mission statement, if not a Rule of Life. A house founded upon the values of my own Community of Aidan and Hilda has Simplicity, Purity and Obedience as its basis. These can be expressed as follows:

> No possessions that clutter the spirit, in order that we live out of God's generosity; no relationships that divide affections, in

order that we live out of God's love; no positions that dishonour another's role, in order that we live out of godly community.

Respect for the patterns of the people who live around, in all things except sin, is a key value. We learned from The House That John Built that early Christians arranged their places of prayer according to the natural patterns of the people. It would be a missed opportunity if those who engine prayer houses repeat the mistake, in a smaller framework, that so many missions and churches have made: to mould those they pray for into their own image. When a particular person or group is fired up to make an impact through their new project, they are tempted to see everything through the eyes of their own egos; instead they should seek to be as Jesus.

Jesus has been described as 'the man for others'. Jesus desires that every person be released to become the unique person he has made them to be. Their physical, emotional and mental being grows into its full stature, and as this happens to more people, the group patterns of the neighbourhood also become more caring, creative – and unpredictable. Jesus calls us to loose people from the things that bind them, not to bind them with our own pietism. For this reason a house of prayer is sensitive to different religious and racial groups. It is also careful not to overshadow other callings – 'let this house decrease and let them increase' is a good prayer. A house of prayer will not drain support from the local church: it is willing to ditch its programme if that is more conducive to the common good.

Creating the right atmosphere is a vital but sensitive task that will be achieved through ongoing reflection. On the one hand, those who come into the house cannot be allowed to do what they like, otherwise users will become prey to the loudest mouth or the biggest ego. On the other hand, if outsiders refrain from coming because they cannot relax and be true to themselves, perhaps because an insecure, schedule-oriented person in charge forces them into their own ways of doing things – then respect and trust, spontaneity and prayer are lost. A prayer house can aspire to be one component in 'a village of God' in which each shines because each is itself.

A prayer house seeks to inculcate a spirit of gratitude for things upon which we depend but too often take for granted: 'Thank you for the engineers of air, wireless, rail and road systems: may their reward be our gratitude,' was a prayer from one house.

Hospitality is a fundamental value. Although no one form of hospitality is essential, the 'hospitality of the heart' is. The context of the Wisdom who builds her house is preparation for the feast to which she is about to invite her guests. It is not an unusual custom in the Old Testament to describe intimate communion with God, and the soul refreshment which people receive under the figure of a festival. Thus, in Exodus 24:11, when the elders of Israel were admitted to the vision of the Almighty, they ate and drank. The same idea occurs frequently in the prophets also (such as Isaiah 25:6; Isaiah 65:13; Zephaniah 1:7, 8), and is brought out in the New Testament in the parables of the great supper (Luke 14) and the marriage of the king's son (Matthew 22). Christ, the supreme Wisdom, has 'built his house' by taking human flesh and also by building for himself a 'spiritual house' (1 Peter 2:5), 'the household of God, which is the church of the living God' (1 Timothy 3:15).

A Celtic prayer, sometimes attributed to Saint Brigid, beautifully expresses this value:

> I would prepare a feast and be host to the great High King,
> with all the company of heaven.
> The sustenance of pure love be in my house,
> the roots of repentance in my house.
> Baskets of love be mine to give,
> with cups of mercy for all the company.
> Sweet Jesus, be there with us, with all the company of heaven.
> May cheerfulness abound in the feast,
> the feast of the great High King,
> my host for all eternity.

Prayer and hospitality are not the same, but they are intimately linked. Both entail opening oneself and one's home to God in the other person. The form this takes can be as varied as are the personalities who host such homes. They may bring the neighbourhood's needs into prayer or offer a weekly shared meal. 'Do not neglect to show hospitality to strangers, for by doing that some have entertained angels without knowing it' (Hebrews 13:2). The American poet Robert Frost wrote that 'home is where they have to take you in.'[33] An ancient Celtic rune suggests ways to express this spirit:

---

33. Robert Frost, 'The Death of the Hired Man' (1914).

We saw a stranger yesterday.
We put food in the eating place,
drink in the drinking place,
music in the listening place,
and with the sacred name of the triune God
he blessed us and our house,
our cattle and our dear ones.
As the lark says in her song:
often, often, often goes the Christ
in the stranger's guise.

Practices

These include a rhythm of prayer. The rhythm will vary. If the owners of a prayer house earn their keep by working office or factory hours, or if they have a family whose school and social commitments dominate, the rhythm will fit round these. If those responsible for the prayer house are set aside to fit other things around prayer, a rhythm of daily common prayer morning, noon and night becomes feasible. My own Community of Aidan and Hilda provides inter-church morning, midday, evening and night prayer patterns for each day of the week and for each Christian and natural season.[34] These are available on CD-ROM and may be downloaded from the internet.

Other communities provide similar patterns. Branches of the universal Church provide their own resources, such as the Catholic *Breviary* and the Anglican *Common Worship*. Most prayer houses also have some kind of programme: a weekly quiet day, intercession hour, meditation or *Lectio Divina* group, quarterly 24-hour prayer activities, for example, as well as prayer activities outside the house.

Structures

In order to find the right structure, questions such as these may be asked:

- How do we best use our premises?
- What common rhythms are we called to?
- What special occasions should we observe?

---

34. Ray Simpson, *Liturgies from Lindisfarne* (Kevin Mayhew Ltd, 2010).

- What open, closed or silent hours should we keep?
- What roles and tasks are required?
- How do we cover for holidays and emergencies?
- How do we review and make policy decisions?
- What are our house rules?

Jesus spoke of his Father's house as having many dwelling-places (John 14:2); he prepares a place that is right for each person. A small terraced house with no garden can be a house of prayer that is like one of these dwelling-places. On the other hand, a larger house with gardens and outbuildings may be able to provide different kinds of dwelling-places. Rooms need to be designated. A garden chalet with easy access might become a silent room. This should be simple and calming with a single focus. Avoid advertising or anything showy. A Bible, chair, table or altar, and a cross or ikon may be enough. The approaches, the outdoors, the furnishings and the connections need to be thought about. Some of the prayer stations referred to in the next chapter could be based in different 'lodging places'.

A human support structure is vital. A full-time prayer house that is not privately owned may need to become a registered charity with trustees, but every prayer house needs support through one or more persons who accompany and affirm those who carry it. L'Arche houses have a spiritual parent who is not part of the work team but who visits often to listen, encourage, identify problems and make suggestions. Community of Aidan and Hilda houses have a soul friend who does something similar. The house gives account to the soul friend who can review with those who carry responsibility for it how the life of the house in the past year has matched up to its aims and values, and how God may be leading it.

In order to find the right values, practices and structures, the sponsors of a house of prayer need discernment. This chapter began by likening a house of prayer to the house that Wisdom builds. Wisdom seeks to understand the constituency it serves. It discerns the spirit of a place. Then it asks, 'What is the prayer house for?' and 'What should be its style?' The answer may come that the prayer house should be anonymous, like a protecting veil over the area; or it may take an up-front style, like the corner shop. It is important to know what God is putting most deeply in your hearts.

Wisdom does not assume that prayer house people 'have it all' – they are part of both the rot and the potential of the area; they are clay in God's hands. A house of prayer is most real when it becomes one with the corruption and dissolution of all things, embraces the web of life, accompanies others into the Unseen Presence so that the Risen Christ accompanies all on their journey.

Prayer house people ask, 'What would the kingdom of God look like here?' They pray it in. They ask, 'What hinders it?' They pray these things out, not by vainly imagined conquest, but by imagining a new way of being a community and praying in transformative goals, resources and relationships.

Dedication of a house of prayer

Saint Aidan of Lindisfarne taught Christians to pray over a site for 40 days before starting to build. We presume the idea was that the spirit of prayer should soak deep into the earth and atmosphere of the place until evil fled and harmonious patterns replaced dysfunctional patterns. If we dedicate, or rededicate, an existing building as a house of prayer, the same principles apply. The person or group God has called to open a house of prayer can walk or sit in it or near it and immerse it in prayer each day. This may be silent awareness of God's presence in that place, inviting the Father to hold it, the Saviour to redeem it, the Spirit to fill it.

When preparations have been made and foundations have been laid, it is good to invite people of goodwill to a dedication of the house, which may include a sharing of its purpose and values, Scriptures, refreshments, prayers for each part of the house and general prayers such as the following:

> We invite Christ to be the host of this household.
> Here be prayer by night and day
> when things go well and when things go badly.
> May the spirit of prayer seep into the very foundations
> until this becomes holy ground.
> **On this holy ground, may friends and neighbours be blessed.**

> May God help each resident and each visitor
> to accept their true path,
> forgive from their hearts,
> and flower as human beings.

Front door
May this house be built upon the Rock of Christ.
May no onslaught undermine it
and no ill wind unsettle it.
May its guardian angel
bless all who enter
and repel all that would harm it.
May Christ to be Master of this house.

Meeting room
Fill this room with a spirit of friendship.
Bless the conversation, the work and the prayer.

Kitchen
We consecrate this kitchen to you.
May the peace of Mary's Son
possess all who work amid its clatter.
May all be done in a spirit of humble service as to you.
Bless the washing.
Inspire the cooking.
Put your glory in the working.

Dining room
Bless this room.
May the eating be a celebration of God's goodness.
May the feasting be a fellowship with God's friends.
As you drink the sweet fruits of creation,
may you drink the sweetness of God's life
and be preserved from the poisons of envy.

Children's rooms
May the loving Father God
always be here with you
and make you feel safe.
May friendly Jesus
always be here with you
and make you feel happy.
May his kindly Spirit
always be here with you

to listen to you.
May you enjoy their company as you play.
May angels look after you when you sleep
and when you dream,
and help you to wake with a smile on your face.

Adult bedroom
In the name of the eternal Father,
in the name of the loving Son,
in the name of the gentle Spirit,
the friendly Three in One:
bless and make holy this room,
and may angels guard all who sleep here.
That part of you that did not grow at morning,
may it grow at night.
That part that did not grow at night,
may it grow in the morning.

Couple's bedroom
God give you delight and tenderness
in your lying together.
God give you peace and forgiveness
in your sleeping together.
God give you space
to be yourselves for each other.

Bathroom or toilets
May all who bathe their bodies here
bathe them in the renewing waters of God.

The sweetness of Christ
as you clean your teeth;
the beauty of Christ
as you comb your hair;
the love of Christ
as you wash your frame.

For the household
May the Kindly Three free each
to accept pain,
to give space to others,
to express feelings,
to forgive from the heart,
to flower as a person.

Back entrance; garden
Dear Lord, may all that is here
reflect the harmony and wholeness
that you want for all your creation.

May the cat(s) purr with the pleasures of friendship;
may the dog(s) wag with the delights of meetings;
may the wild creatures find nature here is friendly;
may the birds find food here and chirp with gladness.

If there is unease about the house's past
Almighty Father,
Victorious Saviour,
Holy Spirit,
you are stronger than the elements,
stronger than the shadows,
stronger than the fears,
stronger than human wills,
stronger than the spirits.
We enthrone you in this place
and lift you up with our praise.

In the name of the crucified and risen Christ,
we set this place free from the power of the past.
In the name of Christ,
we say to all powers that do not reverence him as Lord:
Be gone from this place.

Encircling the whole property
The Caim is said by all:

Circle this place by day and by night;
circle it in winter, circle it in summer.
Look down upon it with your smile;
keep far from it all that harms.
Embrace all within Christ's arms.

May this place be fragrant
with the presence of the Lord.
May this place overflow
with the gratitude of his people.
God's peace be always here,
his likeness in each face.

Chapter 6

Fifty things houses of prayer can do

A house of prayer does not have to 'do' anything; it simply has to be God's heartbeat. It may be God's heartbeat because a contemplative person lives there who breathes the spirit of prayer, often without words, night and day. It may be God's heartbeat because its residents maintain daily prayer; or it may be God's heartbeat because a committed group of activist Christians host a weekly prayer meeting there. Every house of prayer, however, seeks to bring God's kingdom into the area it serves. For this to happen, God's kingdom has first to be imagined. This requires listening, reflection, and all kinds of creative expressions of prayer.

A regular prayer routine is essential, but a prayer house can get into a rut. Praying 24/7 is great, but only if it is an occasional treat; otherwise those who pray can end up more dead than alive. An à la carte menu from which supplicants can create a year's programme or an ad hoc prayer event is a useful aid. The following menu of more than 50 things houses of prayer can do may be placed in a loose-leaf book, so that notes and other ideas can be added. Some will not fit your situation, but they may prompt further ideas that will.

1 – 15: Prayer stations

Prayer stations are a series of visual foci with interactive materials. The pray-ers can spend time at any or all of them and come and go as they please. The stations may be set up for a particular occasion or be a permanent fixture. If they are permanent, they need to be refreshed and changed from time to time. If more than one room or outdoor space can be used, so much the better.

Prayer stations should, as far as possible, cover all types of prayer, such as confession, personal requests, thanksgiving, meditation, acts of devotion, listening, reflection, contemplation, celebration and intercession. Here are some examples of stations:

1. Naming evils

Construct (e.g. with room dividers or bamboo and black cloth) a small prison with two windows. Put a desk inside with paper, pens, metal rubbish bin, candle, matches, basin, jug, towel and some verses from Scripture such as John 8:32; John 8:36; Isaiah 61:1. People are to write on one piece of paper evils or bondages in their societies that hinder knowledge of God, such as selfish pride, greed, prejudice, addiction to drugs, alcohol, sex, pornography, violence. Burn the paper, throw it in the rubbish bin, read and repeat the Scripture verses and wash hands.

2. A cross

Erect a wooden cross and pin to it some Scripture references and a notice such as: 'Jesus on the cross invites you to speak to him. Ask him to reveal anything that you need to confess and be rid of.' Scripture references might include Colossians 2:13, 14; Romans 6:6; Galatians 2:20; 5:24; Matthew 16:24, Isaiah 1:18. Pins and squares of black paper that represent a person's sins are provided. Before leaving, pin a square to the wooden cross.

3. Footprints

Place a sheet on the floor upon which is a large tray or container of sand. Provide sheets of paper and scissors, a chair, and cloths with which to wipe feet before moving to the next station. Display these instructions:

> Remove shoe and sock and place one foot in the sand. If you wish, photograph the footprint. Observe the shape and markings of the footprint carefully. It is unique. Recall that life is a journey, unique to each person.
>
> Stand on a sheet of paper and cut round the shape of your foot. Ask yourself, 'What is the next step of my journey according to God's direction?' Your answer may determine which station you choose next.

4. Reflecting

Place a chair in front of a large mirror. Fix to the edge of the mirror these two sayings: 'Male and female are made in God's likeness' (Genesis 1:27), and, 'The Divine Word is the light in every person' (John 1:4). Place this instruction by the chair:

> Take time to gaze at yourself. As you sit, let go of each negative thought you get about your appearance or character. Keep looking for the beauty of your essence, which is light. How do your feelings begin to change?

5. Throne room

This is a place to sit and reflect on God's character and names, and to worship him for who he is. Scriptures such as Psalm 95:6; Song of Solomon 2:10; Isaiah 55:1; Revelation 4:1 and Matthew 11:28 are to hand. Draped cloths of purple, white and gold set the scene. God's names are written on cardboard. Chairs and cushions, perhaps plants, a fountain and a spotlight add to the royal atmosphere.

6. Reading room

Provide a quiet space where people can sit and read a Bible passage, a psalm or other inspired writings and meditate on what they are reading. Provide a small table, chairs, a bedside lamp, and a selection of Bibles, books or magazines or printed articles.

7. Doing something beautiful for God

Have some beautiful drapes, scents, quiet music, flowers, etc., with supplies of scented oils, incense sticks, candles, matches, sheets of paper, crayons, lavender sprigs and a picture of feet (to represent Jesus' feet) or a picture of Jesus. Have a Bible open at Luke 7:36-47, with the following notice:

> Read Luke 7:36-47. Do something beautiful for God. Place something or a word at the feet of Jesus.

8. Making something out of raw material

Create something like a makeshift potter's workshop. Cover the floor with a sheet. Place two small display tables with plenty of artists' clay on them. Write out and display this Bible verse: 'Yet, O Lord, you are our Father; we are the clay, and you are our potter; we are all the work of your hand' (Isaiah 64:8). Display these instructions:

> Try to shape a person or thing that says something about how you see yourself or someone else as you are now. Place this on the table on the left. Now have a second go, and try to shape it as you or the other person could become with God's help. Place this on the table on the right.

9. Art

Project a changing display of computer pictures of sacred art on to a white wall or screen, or hang a single picture. Rose Windows from Chartres or other cathedrals draw many people. Invite people to gaze at them for as long as they wish to in wordless prayer. Alternatively, a picture painted recently by a local person may be displayed, and the visitor be invited to paint their own picture, or create a Mandala. A Mandala is a circle design symbolising that life is a journey. It is used for meditation purposes. A Mandala can be created by an individual to symbolise their journey by expressing their intuitions in shapes and colours within the circle.

10. Ikons

Place several ikons in an ambient space, and perhaps a large book of ikons. Display instructions such as the following:

> Unlike idols, ikons are windows that lead us more deeply into the divine presence. God desires us to see the invisible through the visible (Romans 1:20). Stand in front of an ikon of a holy person or angel who reflects the divine light and allow this to draw you towards God. Stand with your eyes open and let the ikon 'look' at you. Do not make up your own thoughts; simply allow the divine attribute to which the ikon points fill you. Thus, if it is, for example, an ikon of Christ in glory, we soak in the divine glory. Feel it deeply and allow it to possess and transform you.

Some express the devotion this evokes with a kiss, a bow, a sign of the cross, or a prayer of love.

11. Famous prayers memory gallery

This area could be a traditional room with some of history's most famous prayers inscribed, framed and hung, or it could be a wall or screen onto which such prayers are projected from a computer. As people exit they are invited to test how many they have memorised by writing them down on a blank page of a memory book placed at the door.

A famous one-word prayer is 'Help!' A prayer that millions say every day is known as The Serenity Prayer:

> God, grant me the Serenity to accept the things I cannot change;
> the Courage to change the things I can;
> and the Wisdom to know the difference.

Perhaps the Universal Peace Prayer has overtaken this, since Benedictines, Mother Teresa's sisters, Muslims, Hindus and people of all faiths and none commit to say this daily at midday:

> Lead me from death to Life,
> from falsehood to Truth.
> Lead me from despair to Hope,
> from fear to Trust.
> Lead me from hate to Love,
> from war to Peace.
> Let Peace fill our heart, our world, our universe.

Some prayers are famous because they were spoken by a well-known person before a significant event. This prayer of Sir Francis Drake (d. 1596) is controversial because to England's Queen Elizabeth I he was a legendary and trusted vice admiral in the war against the Spanish, but to the Spanish he was a pirate known as El Draque. He wrote the nub of the prayer in a letter from his ship Elizabeth Bonaventure as it lay at anchor at Cape Sakar on 17 May 1587. Later it was adapted, and in the official form for wartime Britain's National Day of Prayer in 1941 this was attributed to him and became popularly known as 'Drake's Prayer':

Lord God, when you call your servants to endeavour any great matter,
grant us also to know that it is not the beginning, but the continuing of the same,
until it be thoroughly finished, which yields the true glory;
through him who, for the finishing of your work, laid down his life for us,
our Redeemer, Jesus Christ.

In a similar spirit is this much repeated prayer by Ignatius Loyola (d. 1556):

Teach us, good Lord, to serve you as you deserve;
to give and not to count the cost;
to fight and not to heed the wounds;
to toil and not to seek for rest;
to labour and not to ask for any reward,
save that of knowing that we do your will.

The following prayer, although it was not written by Saint Francis of Assisi, is widely known as St Francis' Prayer:

Lord, make me an instrument of your peace;
where there is hatred, let me sow love;
where there is injury, pardon;
where there is doubt, faith;
where there is despair, hope;
where there is darkness, light;
where there is sadness, joy.

O divine Master,
grant that I may not so much seek to be consoled as to console;
to be understood, as to understand;
to be loved, as to love;
for it is in giving that we receive;
it is in pardoning that we are pardoned;
and it is in dying that we are born to Eternal Life.

There may be prayers from different countries, such as this one from Russia:

May I live more simply – like the bread.
May I see more clearly – like the water.
May I be more selfless – like the Christ.

There might be a Prayer of the Month. The gallery can from time to time be rearranged according to topics, seasons, places, church traditions or current needs, and visitors may be invited to leave suggestions.

12. Dining with God

Have a Communion table with a chalice and plate, grapes, red grape juice, bread, candles, matches, chairs or cushions, perhaps fairy lights and quiet, reflective music. Write out and place on the table Scriptures such as Revelation 3:20; Matthew 26:26-8; John 15:5 and words such as: 'Commune in your heart with Jesus and do not leave until you are ready.' Display above the table this poem by George Herbert:

> LOVE bade me welcome; yet my soul drew back,
> guilty of dust and sin
> but quick-eyed Love, observing me grow slack
> from my first entrance in,
> drew nearer to me, sweetly questioning
> if I lack'd anything.
>
> 'A guest,' I answer'd, 'worthy to be here:'
> Love said, 'You shall be he.'
> 'I, the unkind, ungrateful? Ah, my dear,
> I cannot look on Thee.'
> Love took my hand and smiling did reply,
> 'Who made the eyes but I?'
>
> 'Truth, Lord; but I have marr'd them: let my shame
> go where it doth deserve.'
> 'And know you not,' says Love, 'who bore the blame?'
> 'My dear, then I will serve.'
> 'You must sit down,' says Love, 'and taste my meat.'
> So I did sit and eat.

The focus of the following stations should be outward.

13. A prayer requests concourse

Here people are invited to place prayer requests for those in need, for which others can also pray. Provide piles of coloured prayer request slips and pens and an interesting method of displaying these, such as pushing them into coils of chicken wire, hanging them with pegs from string, or placing them in a golden bowl. Spotlights help.

14. News of the world

Project internet world news summaries onto a screen, or place newspaper cuttings on a wall. Have a large notice: 'Pray for these needs of the world' and 'Jesus said, "I will do whatever you ask in my name" (John 14:13).'

15. The four directions

Display a world map or globe and place four different-coloured flags in a holder: Red (East), Yellow (South), Black (West), White (North). Sounds of winds may be played in the background. Display these instructions:

> The flags represent the four corners of Planet Earth: Red (East), Yellow (South), Black (West), White (North). In that order, take the flags and say the following prayers. Pray each of these prayers in turn (some of them echo prayers of Chief Seattle) followed by your own words:
>
> 1) Take the red flag first and face east. 'Great Spirit of Light, come to your children in the east with the power of the rising sun. Never let your children be burdened with sorrow by not starting over again. May hope rise in these I name...'
>
> 2) Face south holding the yellow flag: 'I pray for the people in parched and desert places, for those who lack clean water and green foods, health and opportunities. Send them gentle breezes and rains; send them brothers and sisters who bring provisions and ways of making barren places fruitful...'
>
> 3) Face west holding the black flag: 'Fulfiller of all, I pray to you for all people in the direction of sundown, for those who

feel the sun is setting on their hopes or their life. May they remember that you beckon them to settle down with you. Calm their fears; give them the deep peace of all peace.'

4) Face north holding the white flag: 'All-compassionate One, I pray for people in the north who are cold or icy – give them strength to endure everything that is harsh, everything that hurts, everything that comes.'

16. A regular prayer meal

This combines Scripture and Jewish and Celtic prayers with the sharing of personal stories. It may take place weekly or monthly, or to mark a season. It may include a meal prepared by the host, each person may bring food to share, or it may simply be a symbolic meal of bread and drinks.

If the meal marks the end of the working week, it is an opportunity to gather together the fragments of the week and to be fully present to one another. It can become a household habit to which friends and neighbours come or not, as they wish.

In Jewish tradition, the shabat meal on Friday evening marks Sabbath Eve. Examples of shabat meals are included in *The Heavenly Party* by Michele Guinness.[35]

Some households call this observance a Shalom Meal. The word *shalom*, which is sometimes translated as 'peace', implies personal and communal well-being that is the fruit of living in harmony with self, neighbours, the created world and God.

The following form of words may be varied to suit the house style:

Lord Jesus, be our guest. Stay with us for day is ending.

With friend, with stranger, with young, with old, be among us tonight.

You invite us, Lord, to share with you fragments of our life journeys in the fellowship of a meal.

We keep faith with our God, with those who have gone before us, and with one another, and we give thanks that you provide for your children.

---

35. Michele Guinness, *The Heavenly Party* (Monarch Books, 2008).

Tonight we also thank you for family and friendship, loyalty and love, and that you are present even in setbacks and suffering.

Candles are lit by the host who says:

Light of the world, as we light these candles, may your love shine in our hearts and dwell in our homes, for in your light we shall see light. May we receive the joy that comes from giving and the peace that comes from receiving.

When you have forgiven each other wrongs you do to each other, your Father forgives you.
We forgive each other: we trust that we are forgiven.

Each greets the other with the word shalom or the word 'peace'.

The peace of the Saviour and the saints is with us
Thanks be to God.

Singing, silence or music

We are your guests.
It is you who keeps the generous table.
In trust and friendship and freeing laughter, in food and drink you draw near.

> **Reader** Bread is a lovely thing to eat;
> God bless the barley and the wheat.
> A lovely thing to breathe is air;
> God bless the sunshine everywhere.
> The world is a lovely place to know;
> God bless the folk who come and go.
> Alive is a lovely thing to be;
> Giver of life, we say Bless Thee.
> *Anon*

A loaf is held up

Reader Be gentle when you touch bread.
Let it not lie, uncared for,
unwanted.
So often bread is taken for granted.
There is such beauty in bread –
beauty of sun and soil,
beauty of patient toil.
Wind and rain have caressed it,
Christ often blessed it.
Be gentle when you touch it.
Anon

The bread is passed round and each breaks a piece.
When all have taken a piece, these are eaten.
Then drinks are passed round.

Leader Drink the water of life; renewing our energy; sweetening sour hearts.

Men God creating and strengthening us.

Women God nurturing and sustaining us.

Men Filling us all with the gifts of the Spirit.

Women Flowing through us and setting us free.

All drink.
If there is a full meal, this follows.

Stories are shared. These may be personal experiences of the past week, or they may focus on a theme such as: a lesson learned; a step taken; a fruitful encounter; a discovery made; an evil overcome. Or the story may be told of a person, living or dead, who has inspired personal journeys or whose season it is; those present describe how this speaks to them.

This may be followed by free prayer, the reading of a Scripture to be used on Sunday or singing.

17. Bless a Christmas crib

Let us start before Christmas, when all the world goes into a shopping frenzy only to emerge a month later with debt and hangovers. Make a crib and invite friends and neighbours to join the household in blessing it. St Francis of Assisi said, 'I wish to do something that will recall to memory the little Child who was born in Bethlehem and set before our bodily eyes in some way the inconveniences of his infant needs, how he lay in a manger, how, with an ox and an ass standing by, he lay upon the hay where he had been placed.'[36] So he created a crib with live animals at Greccio.

Prayers such as the following may be said, followed by refreshments:

> Bless this crib. Each time we think of it:
> remind us that you come to us in the ordinary things of everyday life;
> remind us that you are humble, and want to make your home with us.
>
> Homemaker God,
> who made yourself at home in a cowshed,
> may the light of the Bethlehem family
> be a light for us this Christmas.
>
> Universal Child,
> we will welcome you when you call.
> We will open the long-shut parts of our lives.
> We will become young again with you.
>
> The Earth gave you a cave,
> the skies gave you a star,
> the angels gave you a song;
> we will give you our love.
>
> The love that you give us through your Son,
> may we give back to you.
> The love that Mary gave her Son,
> may we give to the world.

---

36. The Catholic Company, 'The Story of St Francis of Assisi and the First Nativity Scene, as told by St Bonaventure'. Available at https://www.catholiccompany.com/blog/story-francis-assisi-first-navity-scene (accessed 3 June 2015).

18. Take a Christmas blessing to each home

Sing carols from door to door either as a house of prayer or by joining with others. Some groups make mince pies in the shape of a crib or give some other delicacy. In parts of Wales they call this custom a *Plygain*. The house may write and produce its own Christmas prayer card. This might feature a photo of its prayer crib. One person wrote this prayer, but you can make yours more personal:

> This Christmas may you be
> humble like Joseph,
> as happy as an angel,
> as generous as the wise men,
> and may the Christmas fuss give way
> to the simplicity of Mary and Jesus.

19. Offer an annual blessing to every house in the neighbourhood

This should be publicised beforehand. Ideally a representative of the house of prayer in each street will sound out neighbours and find out if and when this would be welcome. A personal visit with one or two others is best. The style of the house blessing will vary according to your spiritual tradition. Some may make the sign of the cross over the entrance or give a cross made from something in creation for them to place on a shelf or wall. Others may do a full-blown blessing for each room (see the next chapter). Here is a sample of a prayer than can be printed on a card, but you could make up your own.

> God bless this house.
> Cleanse it from ill, protect it from harm,
> fill it with love and a grateful spirit.
> If there is conflict, let mercy flow.
> Let each day be fresh as the rising sun.

20. Internet praying through tweets, texts, Facebook, blogs

Create a website and a list of neighbours who would welcome you to email, tweet or Facebook them with a prayer each day, week or season. To build up a database is painstaking, but it can be built up naturally through personal interaction over time.

People who come for prayer events may be invited to text their friends a significant prayer. I have set up a Twitter account: #praycelticdaily. Another such account is #morningbell. I tweet one prayer every day and do not use that Twitter account for anything else. If a daily prayer tweet is too much, you could try tweeting a prayer for the week.

Ideally, the prayer tweets rise up in the night, or are stored as inspiration comes, ready to be copied one a day. If inspiration dries up, the house of prayer can retweet favourites from another site. Some popular retweets are:

Today may we dance like fingers on your hand.

Great Spirit, restock our dreams with sacred meaning.

Let us be like trees with deep roots: help us to sustain the land around us.

Gentle Shepherd, deliver us from overdriven leaders. Give us leaders with a limp.

We weep with you for the blindness of pride, the mad rush to consume, the lust to control that drives you from among us.

Come, into the unnamed wildernesses waiting to be unearthed beneath the trivia of our surface lives.

May Christians, Jews and Muslims – all children of Abraham – be like wheat in one loaf.

Teach church people that tradition is to pass on the flame, not to worship the ashes.

May we see the face of Christ in everyone we meet. May everyone we meet see the face of Christ in us.

If 'an honest man's the noblest work of God' (Robbie Burns), then please God make us honest.

The same prayer can be sent via email or Facebook, or posted on a blog. These allow for longer prayers, and pictures.

21. Prayer trees

The concept of a tree of life is a universal symbol of the interconnection of all life. The Bible begins with a tree of knowledge in a garden of innocence, and ends with a vision of a tree of life by a river, which is always bearing fruit and whose leaves are for the healing of the nations (Revelation 22:1, 2). In Celtic Christian spirituality, the Tree of Death, which represents Christ's cross, becomes the Tree of Life through Christ's resurrection. So, in the form of famous large wooden or stone Celtic crosses, the Tree of Death is planted in the soil of the people so that the Tree of Life may take root in the soul of the people.

The custom of placing a wooden or metal tree in a place of prayer is reviving. Prayers are written on slips of card or paper and hung on the tree. This may take one of two forms: prayers that people hang on the tree which are offered to God in a weekly or daily prayer service, or prayers from the praying community that are taken from the tree to the people. This form of praying may focus on a different theme each week. For example, one week the praying community might focus on young people in their area; the next week they might focus on the elderly. The old can pray for the young: 'Send angels, human or heavenly, to steer them away from wasting their young lives.' The young may pray for the old: 'Some drop of grace fall upon them.'

Using the theme of healing leaves, the praying team might each take a leaf and pray for people who have been hurt, or for neighbours who are estranged, or for people who live in an isolated mental frame: 'A leaf for your healing ...'

If the prayer house has a garden beside a public through-way, why not plant a tree with ample branches, or place one in a tub, and invite those passing to tie a prayer to it in the form of a ribbon? Ribbons can be kept in a box nearby. These have no words: they are private to each person who places a ribbon there. The ribbon may carry a specific request, a memory or a 'sorry' for a regretted action or inaction. The winds carry these to the four compass points at different times. Tibetan monasteries in Britain and elsewhere pack people in. They are festooned with prayer flags. Why should Buddhists be the only religious people to do this?

The second type of prayer tree is indoors. It is possible to buy these made of metal, or they may be made of branches tied together. Prayers of intercession or thanksgiving may be written on cards and tied to the tree with string. Daily or weekly, these are prayed for aloud at the household prayer time.

22. Beads, stones or rosaries

Early Christians used beads to ward off distractions and to help them keep an ordered prayer pattern. Some would keep a bowl of beads or stones and hold one in their hand while they made a prayer intention or said a particular prayer, and perhaps repeated it a specific number of times; then they would hold the next bead and repeat the next prayer. Later, such beads were threaded together and worn around the neck or kept in a pocket and were called rosaries. Catholics developed a particular format for the rosary prayer, which involves praying to Jesus' mother as well as to Jesus. Some Christians reject this because they believe we should only address our prayers to God. However, the prayer method of the rosary itself does not require us to pray to Mary. A rosary used to address prayers only to God is becoming known as the Jesus rosary.

Catholic prayer houses will naturally say their traditional rosary. My cousin, Father Kenneth Payne, has written an excellent booklet, *The Rosary Today*.[37] This helps us to recall five Joyful Mysteries (episodes surrounding the birth of Jesus), five Mysteries of Light (episodes that feature Jesus bringing God's kingdom into Judea), five Sorrowful Mysteries (Jesus' suffering and death) and five Glorious Mysteries (Resurrection and Holy Spirit). For each of these 20 mysteries, a brief Scripture leads us into a deep silence of awareness of what the experience that is recorded meant. Out of this awareness we invite God to give to us an affirmation, a gift or a quality of consecration such as was given in the original event. Then, our hearts filled with love for the world that does not know about these things, we ask God to show us how we may apply some insight so as to keep Christ alive in our world. Perhaps we intercede that X may receive an affirmation, that Y may be given grace to bear a cross, or that named groups of people may receive light, challenge, resurrection and so on.

A simpler Bible approach is to paint a Scripture text and a subject for prayer on a stone. Visitors may pick any stone that speaks to their condition and hold it in their hands as they look up the Bible text and

---

37. McCrimmons, 2012.

pray on the theme suggested. A house of prayer might provide stones on which visitors may paint their own text, theme or prayer and take it to their home, school or place of work.

A prayer house may provide a large bowl piled with stones or beads. Or you could try dry bean pods painted different colours. Simple explanations on cards are helpful.

23. Prayer boxes in the supermarket

The prayer house arranges with a local supermarket or corner shop to run a prayer box scheme. As customers exit they see a box or board, plus prayer slips and pencils on which are the words, 'Place your prayer requests here.' A notice explains that these will be placed overnight on an altar at the local house of prayer and offered up at the following Morning Prayer.

24. A prayer map

A useful resource for any prayer house is a large map of the area served by the house. If it is near a population centre, a blow-up of the area which contains facilities such as shopping, education, health, police, religion and leisure should be placed alongside. 'To pray with understanding' requires a sensitive, ongoing process of building knowledge and relationships with as many of these providers as possible. It can begin with any natural link a prayer house member already has with one of these centres. Around the edges of these maps, information that enables more informed prayer can be placed on stickers or in pouches: names of staff or users, perhaps with photos; wrong things that need to be overcome; improvements that would make for greater well-being.

Let us imagine a fictitious superstore named World Empire. It employs people on short-term contracts and pays low wages. Good staff relationships and therefore trust are not attended to. The prices of some products undercut the prices in other shops because their suppliers use child labour or inhumane labour conditions or ecologically damaging processes. The house of prayer could try several approaches. One would be to appeal to the self-interest of the owners or managers and offer to run a free prayer service on the lines of the prayer box suggested in the previous entry. Another approach would be to start praying for the people who are unjustly treated by the shop's suppliers. Then someone from the prayer house might explain to a manager that some shoppers are likely to withdraw their custom – would they consider stocking some fair trade items? Gradually, like yeast in dough, the transformative power of prayer makes itself felt.

25. Prayer walks and trails

Prayer walks can take place anytime, anywhere. They can range from a few friends who are inspired to do an impromptu prayer walk incognito, to a major occasion that involves the whole Body of Christ in an area with a carefully planned route, music, amplification, etc. A prayer house may suggest routes for prayer walks in the vicinity.

Some may benefit simply from the natural joy of being with God in creation. An individual may commune with God as they walk with alert eyes, and bless the terrain by their presence. The house may identify a path which attracts negative energies. Perhaps people fear to go there because violence or thefts have been committed there – the walkers pray for restoration. Or the house may identify a route with landmarks which become prayer stops: a shop, pub, monument, car park, tree, centre, for example.

In contrast to prayer walks, where those who pray are guests on other people's or public land, prayer trails are routes for which the organisers have gained permission to place plaques or signposts. A trail may start at an ambient place such as a church, and indicate the route and distance to the next prayer stop. At each stop a prayer, a Scripture reading, a piece of key information or a meditation is provided. If the stop is indoors, these may be in leaflet form; if outdoors, in the form of a plaque placed in the ground or employing some kind of new technology.

St Teilo's Church, near Abergavenny, decided they did not wish to die and close down; rather they chose to face the challenges of the twenty-first century. So they turned their church building into a warm and welcoming centre, introduced a riverside walk around the church that celebrates nature, and proceeded to develop a Wildflower Walk through the Bible, using stations of a Celtic cross to tell the story of the flower. This relates to the schools' curriculum and contributes to an adult training scheme. I was asked to write a reflection on the Celtic cross that could be used on their quick-response codes. Each signpost has a code which, when photographed by the walker's smartphone, reveals pictures and a meditation. They related the reflections to Acts 17:27, 28, which refers to Christ's presence everywhere and how people might find him as they search for him.

In a city, a prayer or pilgrim trail can link supermarket shoppers to the nearest church, and have stops at places that are significant for the shaping of the past and present of the population. In some cities, groups go on prayer jogs or cycle rides. In my former home city of Norwich, a group of early-morning joggers would stop to pray at each of the city's historic gates.

26. Labyrinths

The labyrinth is a prayer aid. A prayer house can create a temporary labyrinth by using white carpet tape on any floor surface, or outdoors by using a lawnmower to cut swathes between longer grass. Longer-term labyrinths may be made of stronger materials or of stones if outdoors.

The labyrinth is an archetype of our faith journey. It is thought that the Pope urged European cathedrals to develop them as an alternative to pilgrimages to Jerusalem, which became too dangerous during the Crusades. Twenty-two cathedrals had them, most famously Chartres.

Medieval Christian labyrinth designs had two main characteristics. They were based on an equal-armed cross shape. Second, twisting and tortuous paths were used to symbolise a journey to the Holy Land, or the journey Christ took to the cross, or our life's journey to heaven.

So labyrinths are a journey to the 'new Jerusalem', a symbol of God's kingdom. To deepen biblical understanding, look up 'path' or 'way' in a Bible concordance. A labyrinth is not a maze. You can get lost in a maze. With a labyrinth, if you stay on the path you will get 'there'.

The journey can have four stages. Stage one is to be still before we take a first step and ponder a Scripture verse, such as Psalm 25:5. Stage two is to walk the first half to the cross at the centre. As we walk very slowly towards the centre, we offload worries, sins, distractions; we place people or problems we are concerned for into God's hands. We might reflect on 1 Peter 5:7. The third stage is to linger at the centre. Some labyrinths have bread and wine there, to symbolise feasting with Jesus. We might read Luke 10:38-42 and imagine ourselves as Mary sitting at Jesus' feet. We allow God to put whatever he wishes into our hearts. The last stage is the walk back. We visualise ourselves bringing light into the world. We pray for people and situations. We note divine nudges and inspirations. Before we leave the labyrinth we ask God to place a seal over transactions that came from heaven, and that each inspiration received may bear fruit.

There are other ways to use the labyrinth. The classic three stages of mystical prayer can be related to: Releasing (*purgatio*), Reclaiming (*illuminatio*) and Returning (*union*). New Grange, in Ireland, which claims to be the oldest tomb on earth, is a kind of labyrinth. It receives the sun's rays fully on 21 December. In front of the entrance is a stone with spirals. So you begin walking in as though you are dying. You cast away fears and all that holds you down. Later you walk out reborn. Where there is plenty of space, people may chant or dance on labyrinths.

Some labyrinths have circuits of seven and some of eleven, so there is much more to be learned about using these for prayer. The Labyrinth Society is a good source of information.[38]

27. Anniversary celebrations

By keeping ears to the ground, the prayer house may learn of neighbours and friends who have a significant anniversary coming up. Find out if they would like to celebrate with a festive occasion in the prayer house or a barbecue in the garden that ends with prayer and blessings. Keep a calendar of anniversaries of local or national events, and of deaths, weddings, births, etc. of local people. The prayer house might compile a book of graces or blessings on meals, such as the following:

> Bless, O God, this food.
> And if there be anyone who is hungry or thirsty walking outside, send them in to us that we may share this meal with them as you share it with us.

> In a world where so many are hungry, we thank you for this food.
> In a world where so many are lonely, we thank you for this friendship.

---

38. https://www.labyrinthsociety.org/ (accessed 25 April 2015).

May the freshness and fragrance of the farms be with us as we enjoy this meal.
May the freshness and fragrance of your presence linger with us as we journey on.

May this food give new energy to tired limbs, new thoughts to weary minds, and new warmth to cold hearts.

May the blessing of the five loaves and two fishes,
which you shared out among five thousand,
be with us as we eat,
that we may share our renewed lives with a needy world.

You who put beam in golden sun,
you who put food in wheat and herd,
you who put fish in stream and sea,
put a grateful heart in me.

28. A prayer wall

At the Wailing Wall in Jerusalem, pilgrims from all over the world scribble a prayer on a piece of paper and squeeze it into a crack between the stones. If a wall with holes can be built in the prayer house grounds near the roadside, it could be used in this way. At regular intervals, the paper prayer requests will be taken indoors and prayed aloud before being discarded. A prayer wall inside can take the form of rolls of chicken wire or a scratchboard with bricks painted on it. On this, people write their prayer with a felt pen that will rub off after a specified period of time.

29. A litter pick

The prayer house recruits a team, which may include children, to pick up litter in a section of the neighbourhood. The team combines this with prayer for each house, person or thing they pass.

30. Teens days

Local teenagers are invited to bring their smartphones to a special day. They are introduced to the prayer house and invited to visit any of the prayer stations. They are invited to take a selfie of someone praying over them, or of them kneeling before a prayer focus. Samples of memorable prayer tweets are given, which they can text to friends. Each chooses a favourite prayer from many that are displayed, and is recorded reading it out.

31. A thank you a day

Create a year's calendar on a website with daily printouts displayed in the house of prayer. Have a competition. Everyone in the network or area is invited to tweet or email something in their area or life that is worth giving thanks for. Each item of thanks is placed in a vacant day, with the name of the proposer. People are invited to tweet or post 'likes'. At the end of each year the item which received the most thanks is publicised.

32. A street a week

A group may pray along a different street each week, having obtained from the register of electors the names of each resident

33. Prayer concerts

The programme at a prayer concert might include praying in tongues, in silence, in chants and in visualisation. For example, anyone is invited to visualise what changes they see taking place as God's kingdom replaces what currently falls short of that. A concert may include music, laments, praise, arrow prayers shouted out, 'naming and claiming' a promise of God, prophetic prayers expressed in pictures painted on paper, circling prayers, and prayers that use the breath and the body or dance. Alternatively, one theme might be used in each meeting in a rolling programme.

34. Vigils

Vigils may consist of silent, spontaneous or guided prayer. Occasional vigils during a season such as Lent or Advent, or all-night vigils such as on the night of the Passover meal on Jesus' last Thursday on earth, on or on the night when he descended to the world of the dead before Easter Day, accrue added significance.

35. Praying with temperament types

If people do not know about ways of identifying different types of personality, the prayer house might invite qualified people to lead days on Myers-Briggs Personality Tests, the Enneagram or other such disciplines. These can identify styles of prayer that work best for different types. Thereafter the house of prayer might host days or weekends which place people in groups according to their personality and let them try out prayer methods that are likely to be most effective.

A book using Catholic terminology entitled *Prayer and Temperament* sets out suitable ways of praying for four Myers-Briggs Temperament types: Ignatian for SJs, Conversation with God (Augustinian) for NF types, Franciscan for SP and thinking (Thomistic) prayer for NTs.[39] A plenary session when the different groups share can be revealing, and may facilitate people in the work of encouraging one another.

36. Garden and allotment blessings

A prayer house may pray for the well-being of the allotments or community gardens of its members, who invite all their fellow gardeners to join the occasion. Alternatively, the prayer house may be able to establish an annual dedication of allotments. The prayer house itself can display photos of these growing places, with a prayer caption such as, 'May our gardens bear good fruit.'

37. Healing local wounds

To understand the nature, history and varied expressions of wounded group memory and dysfunctional behaviour patterns that may mar some part of a prayer house's catchment area is a calling and a skill that is beyond the scope of this book. Two books that do address this are *Healing Wounded History: Reconciling peoples and healing places* by

---

[39]. C. P. Michael and M. C. Norrisey, *Prayer and Temperament: Different Prayer Forms for Different Personality Types* (revised edition. The Open Door, 1991).

Russ Parker[40] and my own *Healing the Land*.[41] Prayer for the healing of wounds, whether before, during or after a particular process has been engaged in, can only do good if it is free from pre-judgements.

Let us imagine a place that we will call Hard Hill. The people who live there are difficult to get to know and are unwelcoming towards others. Nothing ever seems to change. It is physically a hard place, not only because climbing is hard work (in a different place that might be exhilarating), but also because things of beauty, grace or fruitfulness seem to elude it. The prayer house faithful decide they will meet under the lamp post at the top of the hill and pray for the hardness to be melted. They circle the area with their right arms, and 'melting prayers' flow out of hearts that are kindled by the Undying Flame of Divine Mercy. They think to themselves it would be a pity to let this be a once-only event, but they can't fit repeat group visits into their busy schedules. So they suggest that whenever any of their network passes that lamp post they say a melting prayer.

Hard places come in many guises. In a certain rural area of England, the feudal hold on local patterns remains unbroken. The land-owning class treated tenants as disposable commodities or second-class citizens. A low self-image that vitiates initiative still holds sway long after a particular bad landlord has gone. So the prayer house, taking their cue from Jesus' authorising of his followers to 'bind and release' (John 20:23), binds the sin patterns that were inflicted and releases the image of God that lies unrecognised in the heirs of those who were badly treated.

In another area, the cause of hardness is hostility between groups. These may be two or more villages, streets, families or gangs. In a different area, the hardness is caused by bureaucratic organisations that treat people like cogs in a machine. Both the people who dispense and those who receive the inhuman treatment close and harden their hearts. The prayer house provides faces of people who both run and suffer from the machine. They pray for human relationships that will gradually transform the machine from a tyrant to a tool.

Well-heeled areas can be hard places too, and the worlds of celebrity culture and selfies. Faithful prayer servants pray for a world that is not an extension of self but one in which people look out to others, eager

---

40. SPCK, 2012.
41. Volume 3 of *The Celtic Prayer Book* (Kevin Mayhew, 2004).

for their well-being, and look with wonder to the glories of creation and civilisation. Some may dare, when they pass the ubiquitous selfie, to make the sign of the cross over the selfie-taker, or inwardly bless the selfless part of them that is soul of Christ's soul.

38. Prayer for the unconscious life of the neighbourhood

Chapter three referred to the prayer cell at Bowthorpe that was dedicated to the transformation of the unconscious life of the neighbourhood. An amazing transformation took place that, on the surface, had nothing to do with any visible or audible actions. An altar, corner, chalet, cellar or attic may be dedicated to the transformation of the unconscious life of the neighbourhood, and people may be invited to kneel and hold this intention in their heart.

39. Imagine the kingdom of heaven

Jesus commanded us to repeatedly pray, 'Your kingdom come, on earth as it is in heaven.' A prayer focus can be created with a visual map of the target area for prayer. People are invited to lay hands on one piece of this earth and to pray, 'Your kingdom come, on this piece of earth as it is in heaven.' They then visualise what changes would take place if this bit of earth was as God centred 'as it is in heaven'. They ask:

- What hindrances need to be cleared away?
- What are the weakest links that need to be replaced?
- What creativities need to be unlocked?
- What relationships need to be healed or forged?
- What are the routines, relationships and practices that need to be affirmed?
- What colour needs to be brought in through friendship, sport, music, arts?
- What trust needs to grow in this household or that bank?

An art board can depict both the visualisations and answers to the prayers. A report could be made to civic leaders or the member of Parliament.

40. 1 February – Coming of light/Saint Brigid/Imbolc prayer

Saint Brigid's Day falls on Imbolc, the ancient Celtic first day of spring (in the northern hemisphere) that celebrates the return of light after winter's dark days. A Saint Brigid's cross made of straws or reeds may be placed in homes and outhouses as an extended prayer to repel the dark powers of evil or hunger that may have gained a hold during the winter, and to invite in the light and love of God.[42] Caravans, sheds, boats, wildlife areas, parks, scrubland where gangs hang out – all can be visited.

Traditional churches celebrate this day as Candlemas, and evangelical churches sometimes celebrate a Festival of Light. This prayer that echoes the Jewish Chanukah when candles or other lights are lit may be said:

> Thank you for this beautiful thing named 'light'.
> In it we can observe, act and write, create and feel good.
> May our souls flame forth with the sun's returning glory.
> **As the lights shed their radiance upon us**
> **may they kindle in us the flame of faithfulness,**
> **spur us to struggle more bravely for justice and for truth,**
> **and guide us towards you, the Everlasting Light.**

41. Rogation prayer

The word rogation come from the Latin *rogare*, which means 'to ask'. In the fifth century the French Bishop Mamertus, realising that his city of Vienne was facing disease, fire and attack by wild beasts, established an annual prayer procession in which the entire community pleaded with God to protect them. He is reported to have said, 'We shall pray to God that He will turn away the plagues from us, and preserve us from all ill, from hail and drought, fire and pestilence, and from the fury of our enemies; to give us favourable seasons, that we may have good weather, good health, peace, fertile land and obtain pardon for our sins.'

Churches developed this custom and built four Rogation Days into their calendars. These days are the Major Rogation on 25 April (which

---

42. A video from the Parish Centre at Kildare, Ireland, on how to make a St. Brigid's cross may be downloaded from http://www.icatholic.ie/how-to-make-st-brigid-cross/ (accessed 26 April 2015).

is also the Feast of Saint Mark) and the Minor Rogations on the three days preceding Ascension Thursday. On these days, the congregation would march round the boundaries of the parish and pray for the fields, bless every tree and stone while chanting or reciting a Litany of Mercy. Today Anglicans/Episcopalians tend to pray for fruitful seasons on Monday, commerce and industry on Tuesday, and stewardship of creation on Wednesday, linking this with current environmental concerns.

In rural areas, a house of prayer might revive this practice. In urban areas a walk might be arranged around markets, shops, allotments, gardens and hot spots of pollution. The following may be adapted to suit local conditions:

> Great Spirit, out of your love the universe was born. You have put in place all that is needed for growth and have trusted us to tend it.
>
> Let us ask God to forgive our delusion of self-sufficiency
> and to have mercy on our wasteful lives and wasting earth.
>
> You give this good earth
> but we treat it with contempt.
> Lord, have mercy.
> **Lord, have mercy.**
>
> You give this good earth
> but we squander its finite resources.
> Christ, have mercy.
> **Christ, have mercy.**
>
> You give this good earth
> but we fail to share its bounty.
> Lord, have mercy.
> **Lord, have mercy.**
>
> *Song*
>
> We thank you for the fertile earth, so full of promise. A single seed planted in it can bring forth a hundred seeds.
> **We thank you for light, without which nothing would grow.**
> **We thank you for water, without which plants would wither.**
> **We thank you for air, without which all would die.**

We give you thanks for your ancient promise that while the earth endures, seedtime and harvest, cold and heat, summer and winter, day and night, will never cease (Genesis 8:22).

May creatures and crops grow into well-being.
Happy the people whose God is the Eternal Source.
May our stores be filled with worthy goods.
Happy the people whose God is the Eternal Source.
May our streets be free from clamour and crime.
Happy the people whose God is the Eternal Source.

From Psalm 144

Help us to prepare a way for you
by our thoughtfulness towards the earth,
by our care of crops,
by our upholding of creation.

Show us how to reflect your rhythms in our life
by our tending and consuming cattle and crops with care,
by our work to conserve the world's rich resources,
by giving all creatures their due respect.

Let us look at the soil, look at the seeds, look at what grows, look at the presence of God's Spirit in all of them.

Light of light,
you are here.
Source of water,
you are here.
Breath of life,
you are here.

Silence

Generous God, winter's cleansing cold gave way to spring's gentle warmth, and now summer's sun offers to ripen what we have sown.
Protect this earth from unwelcome predators and untoward elements.

God of compassion, who accompanies your groaning creation from within, have mercy upon the earth.
May all who work the land and sea recognise their dignity and be given dignity.

May all who extract fossil fuels, cut down forests and trawl oceans respect their worth and nature's patterns of renewal.

Bless the seas, rivers and reservoirs.
Teach us to conserve them wisely,
use water sparingly, and share it generously.
May we, who are baptised in water, value every precious drop.

Where earth is parched, and wells run dry;
where war brings want and children go hungry,
give us hands to heal and to plant.

Remind those who are captive to greed, waste and boredom,
and whose harvest is choked by produce that destroys well-being,
that we reap what we sow,
and those who cause harm by mindless habits will also harm themselves.

As the sun circles the world,
circle the land, O God, and the elements above it.
Keep harm without; keep good within.

Circle and bless the seeds ... *(these may be named)*
Circle and bless the fields ...
Circle and bless the tools ...
Circle and bless the work ... the digging and hoeing, weeding and watering, feeding and harvesting ...
Circle and bless the workers ... keep them in good heart.
Circle and bless the crops, *(for example)* the orchards ... herb garden ...
May the sheaves and the greens come in abundance.
Circle and bless the seas and rivers.
Generous be our hearts; open be our hands.
Justice be our goal; thanksgiving be our call.

42. Summer activities

Hold an outdoor barbecue that celebrates summer activities. If possible, obtain permission to do this in a park or public place. Invite donations that enable the prayer house to give free burgers or ice creams. Also hand out stickers with the words, 'The glory of God is seen in a human life lived to the full – God bless your summer activities.'

43. Night life on the streets

The prayer house links up with one of the Street Angels or Street Pastors networks. These walk through urban streets at night when young people are the worse for alcohol, drugs or fights. If the prayer house can offer itself as a base to which injured or frightened people can be accompanied, this may lead to eliciting requests for prayer and enable better follow-up.

44. Harvest-time tents

In the Old Testament, as I recalled in chapter one, Jews created booths made of branches in which they lived for a week during harvest time, which they called the Festival of Shelters. In some Jewish quarters, tents are erected in gardens to fulfil a similar purpose of moving outside the familiar comfort zone in order to be more aware of dependence upon Providence. This Jewish holiday is celebrated on the fifteenth day of the month of *Tishrei* (this varies from late September to late October). The holiday lasts seven or eight days.

A house of prayer can organise a list of young people and the young at heart of all ages who erect tents or huts made of branches. It may provide printouts of prayers that the adventurers may say before they sleep.

Each participant picks and holds up a branch or twig and all say this blessing together: 'Blessed are you, O Lord our God, King of the universe, for keeping us in life, for sustaining us, and for helping us reach this day.'

They make a procession and say a prayer known as *Hoshanos*. It is a prayer for God's blessing. Anyone may mention something upon which they call down God's blessing and everyone says *hoshana*, meaning 'save now'.

45. Remembrance

November is a time to remember forebears, war dead and deceased loved ones. Some crematoria and churches hold special services on 2 November, All Souls' Day, or on the nearest Sunday. Beforehand they invite people to write the names of loved ones who have died in the last year or so in a book. During the service each name is read out and a candle lit and placed in their memory. Then there are prayers.

A house of prayer may host a service in areas where no such service is held. In areas where a service is held, the house of prayer can support it by having a loose-leaf Book of Remembrance and taking it to the service. It can then dedicate a space where candles in remembrance of loved ones may burn afterwards, and to which relatives are invited. A prayer such as the following may be placed on an altar:

> The seed is Christ's; the granary is Christ's.
> In the granary of God may we be gathered.
> The sea is Christ's; the fishes are Christ's.
> In the nets of God may we all meet.

46. New Year

In recent years, Hogmanay or New Year celebrations with fireworks and partying have edged out the traditional practice of a Watchnight Service. A house of prayer might try to combine the two. An hour's prayer vigil could precede or follow the festivities. The service may include prayers of dedication for the coming year, and a period of silence during which people write down God's priorities for them and make resolutions.

A bell may be rung. Verses from Alfred, Lord Tennyson's 1850 poem might be read, such as:

> Ring out the old, ring in the new,
> ring, happy bells, across the snow.
> The year is going, let him go;
> ring out the false, ring in the true.
> Ring out the grief that saps the mind,
> for those that here we see no more,
> ring out the feud of rich and poor,
> ring in redress to all mankind.
> Ring out a slowly dying cause,

and ancient forms of party strife;
ring in the nobler modes of life,
with sweeter manners, purer laws...
Ring out false pride in place and blood,
the civic slander and the spite;
ring in the love of truth and right,
ring in the common love of good...
Ring out the darkness of the land,
ring in the Christ that is to be.

47. Three 40-day periods of prayer intentions

Christians observe the 40 weekdays before Easter as a season of reflection, penitence and preparation for the celebration of Christ's resurrection. They call this season Lent. The Bible tells of God-guided people who dedicate 40 days to seek God. Moses did it before he received the Ten Commandments; Jesus did it before he began his public ministry. Early churches in Britain and Ireland developed three seasons like Lent. The other two were the 40 days before Christmas and the 40 days after Pentecost.

This is a tool that prayer houses can usefully adopt even if they are not part of a church that observes church seasons. Prayer houses can make known that the house will be observing these special 40 days of prayer, and provide a prayer intention and an action for each day to those who come to the prayer house. These can be emailed to those who wish to use them elsewhere.

During Advent, it is a custom to visualise the coming of Christ into the world in judgement and mercy and to 'pray in' this coming – not only ultimately but as first signs now. Hence many prayers begin with the word, 'Come'. On one day we might pray that Christ the Justice Restorer (Judge) will come and remove things that mar our neighbourhood, and on another day that Christ the Fulfiller will bring to fruition incipient possibilities for good that we have identified.

During the 40 days before Easter the prayer theme might be preparing a way for God to move among us. Pray that things that oppose God may be cleared out, and that messes may be cleared up.

During the 40 days after Pentecost it is good to pray that the flame-like Spirit that alighted on the first disciples at Pentecost may alight on each person they pray for, or that one of the fruits of the Spirit may grow in them. We gave the theme 'Walking in the Spirit' to one 40 days of prayer after Pentecost. Each day a stone was held in the hand and laid down. The theme of the first week was 'Let God cleanse us'. On the first day we took and laid down the stone of pride, abandoned ourselves to God without conditions and said, 'I lay down my pride.' Each day of the first week focused on one of the seven deadly sins. Week two focused on evils in the locality and week three on praying in the matching virtues. Week four was for the healing of the locality, and in week five we prayed in one of the seven fruits of the Holy Spirit, and so on.

48. Up to ten-day periods of seasonal prayer intentions

The idea of periods of prayer intentions can be adapted to shorter periods of time. For example, over the Twelve Days of Christmas we might pray or sing, 'O Come Let Us Adore Him' or 'Come here and live among us'. During Epiphany (the spreading of Christ's light to new places), we might pray for the light of transparency to come into places of shady dealing as well as for a better understanding of Jesus to dawn upon people in schools and faith communities. After Easter, the prayer house may invite users to pray for the world through the resurrection eyes of Jesus:

> Risen Christ, you burst from the grave: now burst into life through us.
> Risen Christ, you revealed yourself to Mary in a cemetery garden at dawn. Reveal yourself to us in the dawnings of our lives.
> Risen Christ, you revealed yourself to Thomas when he felt the scars in your body. Reveal yourself to us as we touch the scars of the world.
> Risen Christ, you revealed yourself to two walkers as they welcomed you into their home. Reveal yourself to us as we walk and open our homes.
> Risen Christ, you revealed yourself to the fisherfolk as they toiled in vain at their work. Reveal yourself to us in our long hours of toil.
> Risen Christ, you revealed yourself to many as they met beneath the open skies. Reveal yourself to us in the spacious grace of creation.

During the season of Trinity, pray that Christians may fall in love with the Three Loves eternally communing in the heart of God, and that the institutions and patterns of the world may reflect the divine Relationship that is the true model for society.

In the last period of this yearly cycle, the focus can turn to the 'cloud of witnesses' who urge us on in the race of our lives (Hebrews 12:1). One or two God-guided personalities may be recalled. Encouragement, perseverance and the prize of heaven become our themes.

49. Intercession blitzes

According to one dictionary, a blitz can mean 'a concerted effort to deal with something'.[43] As a young man I was put off intercession because I felt that loud-mouthed Christians used prayer meetings to impose their agendas on everyone else. Appropriately used, however, intercession is an essential string in the bow of prayer.

Intercessors have been likened to the gatekeepers recorded in the Old Testament who kept watch over the temple or the city. They were given certain tasks. There is a place for a group of people coming together to storm the gates of heaven. The Church at Antioch included many prophets and teachers who had tasks and who met to intercede. They prayed for particular needs and for people to be raised up by God who would respond to those needs (Acts 13:1-4). That is how Saul and Barnabas came to be sent out on their great missionary endeavours. 'In everything by prayer and supplication with thanksgiving let your requests be made known to God,' wrote Saul who became known as Paul (Philippians 4:6).

No one should feel pressured to attend intercession meetings. Those who do attend may put up lists of significant prayer targets and key words, thoughts and pictures that seem to relate to these intercessory targets. The Christian New Testament scholar Walter Wink asserted that 'history belongs to the intercessors'.[44]

50. Local organisations prayer link-up

The prayer house compiles a list of every organisation, institution and network in their overview. They may either pray for one each day, or

---

43. *The Oxford Advanced Learners Dictionary*.
44. Walter Wink, cited in James K. Beilby (ed), *Understanding Spiritual Warfare* (Baker Academic, 2012).

dedicate a specific day each week or month for this purpose. Before or after, they email each organisation to include a reply form for prayer requests to be indicated and/or to inform them that they have been prayed for.

51. Emmaus walks

An Emmaus walk is a biblical meditation undertaken with another person. Luke 24:13-25 describes how Jesus, after he had been killed and raised to life, joined two disciples while they walked to the village of Emmaus. At first they did not realise who he was, but as they walked and talked together their hearts burned within them, and he opened their minds to understand the Bible.

The two modern walkers choose a sacred site or a renewing place to walk to, a mile or more from their starting point. They talk on the outward journey and are silent on the return journey. They meet at the starting place (a quiet place) and decide on a topic that they think God might want to speak to them about – but do not focus on a problem as such. They choose a suitable Bible passage. Some resonant passages are Matthew 4:1-11; 4:18-25; 5:1-14; 5:38-48; 6:24-34.

Before they depart they settle into a relaxed silence, then pray in their own or these words: 'Risen Christ, open our eyes to your presence, open our ears to your call, open our hearts to your love. As the hearts of the Emmaus walkers burned within them, so may our hearts burn within us as we walk and talk with you.' They read aloud the Bible passage, and perhaps a commentary on it from a book or their own knowledge, followed by five minutes of silence.

As they walk, they prayerfully share thoughts or questions that come out of the reading, although they should feel free to move into other areas if led. They only speak when they are moved to by God, to recall any historic or natural inspiration the place evokes, and silently or aloud to welcome Jesus afresh into their lives. They may wish to share bread or light a fire.

They retrace their steps in silence unless there is something they are bursting to say. There should be an openness of heart and mind to the Lord and one another, in simple awareness of the Lord's presence. On their return to the starting place they may reread the Bible passage. In silence they recollect what has been most significant in their walk. After five minutes they may share this, but not have a discussion.

They conclude with a prayer such as this: 'Lord, thank you for your presence with us on our pilgrimage, for our time together and for all we have received from you. Help us to carry your healing presence to our sisters and brothers, and ever to walk with you. The grace of our Lord Jesus Christ, the love of God, and the fellowship of the Holy Spirit be with us always.'

Chapter 7

Prayers that bless the world around

In Jewish tradition, the *Berakhah* is a blessing that draws down spiritual energy. It is usually a formula recited at certain occasions. Its purpose is to acknowledge God as the source of all blessing and to bring awareness of God into everyday occurrences. A *Berakhah* typically starts with the words, 'Blessed are you, Lord our God...' and those who hear it say, 'Amen'. The *Berakhah* may be said before food, before lighting a Sabbath candle, upon seeing an awesome sight or upon hearing very good or bad news.

Christians enlarge this principle of blessing. God blessed the consummation of everything in creation (Genesis 2:3). Jesus blessed infants as well as bread, crowds as well as friends. He even asked his disciples to bless those who persecute them (Luke 6:28). The author of 1 Peter 3:9 wrote, 'Repay [abuse] with a blessing. It is for this that you were called – that you might inherit a blessing.' Christ's final act on earth was to bless his assembled disciples (Luke 24:50), and before that he affirmed them in continuing his work of binding and loosing (blessing) (Matthew 18:18). 'To the pure all things are pure' (Titus 1:15) and every blessed thing can be blessed.

Perhaps the most famous blessing in the Bible is that of Aaron upon his people:

> The Lord bless you and keep you;
> the Lord make his face shine on you and be gracious to you;
> the Lord turn his face toward you and give you peace.
>
> *Numbers 6:24-6 (NIV)*

What follows is an A–Z selection of prayer tasters for a cross section of people and places. You and your prayer house colleagues can allow these to trigger extended free prayer or perhaps write your own prayers based on local knowledge. Each prayer house could have a loose-leaf folder labelled A–Z to which new entries may be added and from which overdone entries may be deleted or parked for a time.

Abused women or men
O God our Desire, you formed us in our mother's wombs and call us by our names.
May these dear ones know that you can make their violated bodies vessels of love.
Draw forth the divine beauty in women *(men)* who feel degraded
and in men *(women)* who abuse their role.

Babies
May each human life be cherished from conception to the grave.
A little drop of your Creator fall upon you, little one.
A little drop of your Saviour, and a little drop of the Spirit
to bless you with goodness and calling
and bring you to fullness of life.

Children
Jesus,
bless their eyes – so they notice others;
bless their hearts – so they love others;
bless their hands – so they help others.
Teach them to
explore your world,
learn from mistakes,
use their talents,
remember what matters
and grow to be like you.

Dying residents
May you journey towards the heart of God,
be kept in his love and be healed of bitter memories.
May you journey towards the heart of God,
free as the wind, and straight as an arrow.

The seed is Christ's; the granary is Christ's.
In the granary of God may you be gathered.
The sea is Christ's; the fishes are Christ's.
In the nets of God may we all meet.

Ethnic groups

Father, from whom every family in heaven and on earth draws its essential character.
We name these ethnic groups in our area...
In them may goodness, trust and achievement flourish.
May those things which demean or hinder your kingdom die away.

Families or households

God bless them.
May they
express their needs,
forgive from their hearts,
accept each other's pain,
enjoy each other's company,
flower as people,
and reflect a little bit of heaven in their homes.

Fitness

We pray for our population to have healthy bodies, minds and souls.

God make us fit for purpose,
alive in heart and limb.
God stretch our creaking bodies
till they tingle and feel trim.

Put fibre in our being;
take flabbiness away.
Strengthen what is weak;
keep binge and bulge at bay.

May each body be a temple
of your Spirit, who is true;
a picture frame on earth
of eternity on view.

Gangs

We name these gangs in our area . . .
Where they need affirming, bring enablers alongside them.
Where they need boundaries, give courage to those who can make them effective.
Plant in their hearts fresh seeds of possibility.
Draw them into your love.

Holidays

We pray for all who are on holiday.
Blessing of discovery be yours,
and blessing of rest.
Blessing of scenery be yours,
and blessing of sleep.
Blessing of meeting be yours,
and blessing of solitude.
Blessing of fun be yours,
and blessing of thought.
Blessing of change be yours,
and blessing of homecoming.

Industry

Spirit of God, among the wheels of industry,
renew the face of the earth.
May the wealth and work of the world
be available to all and for the exploitation of none.
May employers, employees and shareholders
work together like fingers on a hand for the common good.

Internet addicts

Lord, speak to those who are downloading trivia, horror or porn.
Download heavenly spaces where you may be born in them anew.

Justice

God from whom all truth and justice flow,
may justice be something that cannot be bought.
We pray your justice for people mistreated, for those robbed of their basic human necessities or treated unfairly by those in authority ...
We plead for your justice to fill all the lands
as the waters cover the sands.

Leisure pursuits

We pray for all who take leisure this day:
blessing of activity be yours and blessing of rest;
blessing of scenery be yours and blessing of thought;
blessing of entertainment be yours and blessing of sport;
blessing of meeting be yours and blessing of food.
Make whole the leisure of this day.
Restrain its hostile impulses and fill its moments.

Media

May the media draw out the glories and tragedies that lie beneath the world's surface trivia and interpret reality's many facets to the peoples of the world.
Remind everyone who uses social media today to be mindful.
Protect naïve users from abuse, bullying and ugly attitudes.
Help us to redeem the media so it becomes a source of blessing and not a curse.

We pray for all our Facebook friends ...

Medical centres, surgeries and hospitals

God of wholeness,
may they not be centres of disease but centres of healing.
May they not treat cases but make people whole.
May many grow well, others die well, and staff work well.
Through Christ the Great Physician,
inspire us to create person-centred health care and to refuse to shuffle patients like numbers on a computer.

Nightlife

We pray for all those who will engage in the nightlife soon to begin.
Circle them, Lord; keep harm without; keep good within.
Help them discern the difference between fashion and true friendship;
between addiction and true freedom.
Give them the graces of meeting, restraint and joy.

Circle the nightclubs, Lord.
Keep harm without; keep grace within:
grace of movement and grace of restraint;
grace of integrity and grace of meeting.

Offices

Bless those offices and work spaces that touch so many people.
Grace all who work in them to speak your peace and order into their atmosphere.
May they manage well the tasks of this day;
may the papers be well kept;
may unnecessary things be brought to their end;
may each call and text have a welcoming tone.

Old people

All-seeing One, teach them that ageing is inevitable and maturing is still an option.
All-compassionate One, teach them to cease trying to give what they can no longer give, but to give all that they have to give – with love.
All-attractive One, as we grow old, may we become less like creaky, complaining vessels and more like vintage wine.

Parents

Through their wisdom may their children learn to know right from wrong.
Through their tenderness may their children learn to trust, to explore, to care.

Parks and play areas
We pray for these parks...
Inspire those who tend them to make them beautiful, peaceful or interesting places.
We pray for these play areas...
Inspire those who maintain and those who use them
with a spirit of fun, friendship and care.
We pray for public spaces.
Help us as residents to value them as breathing or wild spaces,
but not as dumping places.

Partners
May they be a strength in need, a comfort in sorrow, a companion in joy,
and become your partners too.

Police
Help our police to be good public servants, to be honest and free from prejudice,
to desire that wrongs be put right, that victims be taken seriously,
that law-breakers be disciplined without malice, and given hope of reform.

Quarrels
We pray for these households, groups or streets that are caught up in quarrels...
Bring into their limited horizons the possibility of better ways.
Bring into their situation conflict resolvers and trust builders.

Religious groups
We pray for these we know from other faith traditions...
We pray for the mosque, temple, synagogue or...
Bind us together in the common pursuit of goodness and truth.
May we look upon one another not as strangers but as pilgrims together.

Schools

May our schools feed minds and nourish character, teach courage and respect, joy of achievement and service, and the interconnectedness of all things;
may they not just churn out units of production.
May pupils and staff, governors and parents be a learning community.

Shops

May our shops meet true need, stock worthy goods, honour all in the supply chain, treat staff well, and be a blessing to their customers.

Sick people

Lord, there is so much disease.
Some is inevitable, but so much is caused by addiction, worry,
and unhealthy habits that create dis-ease.
Lead your troubled children from dis-ease to calm, from denial to acceptance,
from fragmentation to wholeness.

Singles

Help them bring their deepest longings to you.
May they find joy in opening themselves to you in all that this day brings.
May they find healing if past hurts have weakened their ability to trust.
May they journey in your life-giving calling,
whether these are to solitude or achievement, friendship or service.

Sports

May running and jumping praise you;
may swimming and cycling praise you;
may teams and contestants praise you.

Bless to them their bodies;
bless to them their brains.

Bless to them their training;
bless to them their games.

Free these sports from prejudice, bribery and ill will.
May fun, fitness and fellowship flourish.

Theatres, cinemas, galleries, concert halls
Lord, false conditioning often veils you from the sight of people who are made in your likeness.
May truth, goodness and beauty be fully utilised to remove that veil.
We pray especially for these places, that fresh perspectives, deeper seeing, laughter that frees or human angst that develops empathy
may break through into the lives of those who visit them.

Transport
We pray for our streets – the vehicles, drivers and passengers who pass along them;
the buses, cars and taxis, the delivery vans and cycles.
We pray for our railways, the passengers and staff.
We pray for the aeroplanes above us.
Help everyone to be mindful and to travel with you.

Unemployed people
Remind them, Lord, of their worth to you.
Give them, Lord, things to do:
talents to use, people to cheer,
lessons to learn, nothing to fear.

Vocations
Triune God who mothers us all,
we pray for those who have not found or who feel thwarted in their vocation.
Call into being nurturers of those who search.
Foster fresh callings.
We pray this for these whom we hold in our hearts...

Work

Rekindle a joy and faithfulness in work.
May the wealth and work of the world
be available to all and for the exploitation of none.
May employers, employees and shareholders
work together like fingers on a hand for the common good.
May customers, suppliers and fellow staff honour one another.

(E)xams

Spirit of truth and consolation, give those who have exams
wisdom to know the nub of things,
strength to recall what is useful, and
peace to leave the result to you.

Young people

Help these young people
not to doubt their value or run from whom they are.
Help them to grow in confidence
and find affirming adults to be alongside them
to unplug from futile distractions
and plug into the Source of well-being.

Zingers (outstanding persons or things)

Thank you for the zingers in our midst:
those who make things happen, gain our admiration, raise morale or entertain us
even when things are grey.
In particular, we pray for these who help to shape our civic, social, working and leisure lives...
Give us God-guided personalities who make for God-guided localities.

And finally...

Let us liberally sprinkle this Celtic 'mother of all blessings':

May the blessing of light be on you, light without and light within.
May the blessed sunlight shine on you like a great peat fire, so that stranger and friend may come and warm himself at it.
And may light shine out of your two eyes like a candle set in the window of a house, bidding the wanderer come in out of the storm.
And may the blessing of the rain be on you, may it beat upon your Spirit and wash it fair and clean, and leave there a shining pool where the blue of heaven shines, and sometimes a star.
And may the blessing of the earth be on you, soft under your feet as you pass along the roads, soft under you as you lie out on it, tired at the end of the day; and may it rest easy over you when, at last, you lie out under it.
May it rest so lightly over you that your soul may be out from under it quickly, up and off and on its way to God.
And now may the Lord bless you, and bless you kindly.

Conclusion

As I have reflected on a life-changing encounter I had in a cowshed on the Holy Island of Lindisfarne, it has seemed to me that God is saying, 'Let's replace those churches that are monuments with a myriad little Bethlehems.' They may be transitory, but they are homely and transforming, and here the mother and the lover, the poor and the rich will be drawn to pray. That is the spirit of a new prayer-house movement.

We can hardly underestimate the effect of such a movement, as this ancient saying so beautifully expresses it:

> If there is righteousness in the heart,
> there will be beauty in the character.
> If there is beauty in the character,
> there will be harmony in the home.
> If there is harmony in the home,
> there will be order in the nation.
> If there is order in the nation,
> there will be peace in the world.

When I travel to places such as Kuala Lumpur, I usually arrive on a weekday. I see the occasional church notice board. This tells me that there are one or two services on a Sunday, but I will have left by then. I return to my sleeping quarters and am woken up by a call to prayer from a minaret. This highlights the need for Christianity to restore daily prayer in public places. Could some houses of prayer in areas where this would not be culturally alienating offer a daily call to prayer by bell or digital means?

Although The House That John Built may have disappeared from sight centuries ago, John's inspiration remains among us. The universal Church celebrates John's life every year on the third day of Christmas. 'We know love by this,' John the loved disciple writes in his first letter: through our obedience to the Father, our trust in Christ and our abiding in the Spirit (1 John 3:16, 24; 4:7).

An underlying theme of this little book – discovering God in our familiar patterns – is grounded in a Johannine theology. Half the world is Monist: Ultimate Reality is One, whether it be Isness (Buddhists), God (Muslims) or Big Bang (Atheists). This means that there is just 'I', no 'We'. Human beings, therefore are a collection of 'Is', not 'We'. Jesus revealed God to us, however, as other-centred, not self-centred. God's heart is Relationship, not Rule; not Mono but Triune. Or, as Ellis Potter expresses it in his *Three Theories of Everything*, 'God alone is God: God is not alone'.[45] Original perfection is objectively one God and subjectively Three-in-One – a communion, a home into which we are invited.

The New Testament invites all humans into a fellowship with God. The central image of God's kingdom is a feast. The central feast of Christianity is called Holy Communion. We could say that God has a homing instinct which is also the deepest instinct in human beings.

Prayer is the cry of the heart. As we cry from the heart we are drawn into God's heart – the communion of love. God becomes our home. As our homes become places of human heart cries, Christ becomes at home with us.

---

45. Ellis Potter, *Three Theories of Everything* (Destinee Media, 2012).

Books by Ray Simpson to resource prayer houses

Published by Kevin Mayhew Ltd:

Prayer Rhythms for Busy People: A Pocket Companion (1500775)
Daily morning, midday, evening and night-time prayers

Ray Simpson: His Complete Celtic Prayers (1501278)
More than 1500 prayers to reconnect us with the streets and the seasons, the Scriptures and the saints, the struggles and the silence. The exhaustive index enables users to find a prayer for every occasion.

Liturgies from Lindisfarne: Prayers and services for the pilgrimage of life (with CD–ROM) (1501225)
This provides prayer services for the days of the week, the Christian festivals, natural seasons, creation, healing and special occasions.

The *Gift Prayer Book* Series

The *Celtic Prayer Book* in four volumes

For details of all Ray Simpson's books, please see our website: www.kevinmayhew.com

And to resource larger churches that aspire to be spiritual homes of prayer:

The Transforming Church Course
An all-age programme of 11 units that can be engaged with monthly or weekly by midweek church groups and on Sundays. The units explore creation care, life-long learning, listening prayer and villages of God.